Nationalism, Marxism, and African American Literature
between the Wars

Nationalism, Marxism, and African American Literature between the Wars

A NEW PANDORA'S BOX

Anthony Dawahare

University Press of Mississippi   Jackson

Margaret Walker Alexander Series in African American Studies

www.upress.state.ms.us

An earlier version of chapter 5 was published as "Langston Hughes's Radical Poetry and the 'End of the Race'" in MELUS 23.3 (fall 1998). An earlier version of chapter 6 was published as "From No Man's Land to Mother-Land: Emasculation and Nationalism in Richard Wright's Depression-Era Urban Fiction" in *African American Review* 33.3 (fall 1999).

Print-On-Demand Edition

⊗

Library of Congress Cataloging-in-Publication Data

Dawahare, Anthony, 1961–
    Nationalism, Marxism, and African American literature between the wars : a new Pandora's box / Anthony Dawahare.
        p.   cm. — (Margaret Walker Alexander series in African American studies)
    ISBN 1-57806-507-0 (cloth : alk. paper)
    1. American literature—African American authors—History and criticism.   2. Nationalism and literature—United States—History—20th century.   3. Communism and literature—United States—History—20th century.   4. Socialism and literature—United States—History—20th century.   5. Black nationalism—United States—History—20th century.   6. American literature—20th century—History and criticism.   7. African Americans—Intellectual life—20th century.   8. African Americans—Politics and government.   9. African Americans in literature.   10. Black nationalism in literature.   11. Politics in literature.   12. Race in literature.   I. Title.   II. Series.
PS153.N5 D34 2002
810.9'896073—dc21   2002006910

British Library Cataloging-in-Publication Data available

To Tillie Olsen and her generation of activists from the 1930s—
"strong with the not yet in the now"—who struggled tirelessly for
an egalitarian world free from racism, sexism, and class oppression.

To my children, Wyatt and Hannah, who have better worlds to make.

Contents

Acknowledgments

I would like to thank Barbara Foley for her careful reading of the manuscript; her insights helped to refine several ideas on both African American literature and the interwar American Left. Thanks to Joseph Skerrett, former editor of MELUS, who published an earlier version of chapter 5 and assisted (perhaps unknowingly) in fine-tuning ideas I presented from chapter 6 at a MELUS conference. Sincere thanks to Bill Mullen and James Smethurst for their valuable comments on chapter 2 and their stimulating conversation over the years on African American literature and the Left. I am also indebted to Houston A. Baker Jr., whose summer seminar on "African American Voices: Language, Literature, and Criticism in Vernacular Theory and Pedagogy" (Pennsylvania State University, College Park, June 21–25, 1994) helped to shape my comprehension of black literature and theory. My understanding of the culture and politics of the 1930s benefited from an NEH Summer Institute I attended in 1995 at the University of North Carolina, Chapel Hill, entitled "The Thirties: American Literature, Art, and Culture in Interdisciplinary Perspective." The biannual working-class studies conference at Youngstown State University's Working-Class Studies Center never failed to enrich my appreciation of working-class culture and politics. California State University, Northridge, provided me with vital reassigned time to conduct research for this project. The Southern California Library for Social Studies and Research, under the direction of Sarah Cooper, made available indispensable archival materials on the American literary and political Left. Many conversations with my longstanding friend Ralph Leck have undoubtedly influenced my own view of the importance and function of critical theory. Heartfelt thanks to my parents, Victor and Helen Dawahare, whose daily labors have helped to shape this writer's confidence in the working class. And, finally, profound thanks to Krista Walter, my intimate companion, whose indefatigable standards for critical thinking and writing have enriched this project in more ways than I can express.

Introduction

Every minority and suppressed group seeks self-expression. Woodrow Wilson let off the lid of a new Pandora's box when he so eloquently preached this doctrine as the shibboleth of the war. The Negro seeks self-determination also.

Kelly Miller, "The Harvest of Race Prejudice" (1925)

Hopelessness is itself, in a temporal and factual sense, the most insupportable thing, downright intolerable to human needs. Which is why even deception, if it is to be effective, must work with flatteringly and corruptly aroused hope.

Ernst Bloch, *The Principle of Hope*

Marxism and nationalism constitute two of the most influential ideologies of the last century. They have generated many cultural and political movements worldwide and have radically transformed conceptions of self, culture, and society in the modern period. The goal of this study is to evaluate the great impact of Marxism and nationalism on a relatively small segment of writers from the twentieth century, particularly black writers from the Harlem Renaissance and the Depression-era proletarian literary movement. Living during those tempestuous years of economic crisis and war, many black writers found common cause with nationalist and internationalist ideologies and movements that spoke to their own desires for social equality. The "new Pandora's box" contained the hope that self-determination was still possible, in spite of the many disappointments bred by a history of slavery, segregation, and racism. Indeed, the twenty years between the wars were two of the most politically productive and culturally rich decades of the twentieth century for African American writers.

Yet, like the old Pandora's box, the new one also contained a mess of social evils that were set free during this period, and not only by Woodrow Wilson. My principle argument in this book is that the spread of nationalist ideologies and movements during the interwar period, culminating in the Nazi genocide, functioned for a time to divert the legitimate political desires of many black writers for a world without racism along channels that did not throw into question the capitalist foundation of modern racism. Seduced by the promises of the ethnic nationalism of the period, most Harlem Renaissance writers replicated in their literary work many of the pseudo-scientific notions of racial and national identity that capitalism had used since its inception in the United States to deflect attention away from the class basis of exploitation and inequality. I also argue that the strongest black writers of the period are precisely those who did not heed the call of nationalism and were, on the contrary, receptive to the internationalist ideas of the American and European Left. Understanding that receptivity implies availability, I demonstrate that it is during the "Red Decade" that black writers developed some of the sharpest critiques of nationalism. Black Communist writers, as well as their white comrades (most of whom are out of the purview of this study), historically anticipate a growing body of contemporary scholarship that reveals the intellectual vapidity and political hazards of nationalism, especially its ability to generate feelings of grandeur in return for the working class's cooperation in an exploitative peace or an imperialist war. This study, therefore, challenges a reigning paradigm in black literary studies that privileges the cultural nationalist writings of the Harlem Renaissance as the most relevant literature of the interwar period.

While I work to demonstrate the dominance of nationalism in the 1920s and Marxism in the 1930s, I also address the ways in which these ideologies coexist in the movements of both decades. That is, on the one hand, throughout the interwar period, Marxism and nationalism confront each other as antagonistic phenomena. Nationalistic texts of the 1920s polemically engage those of Marxism, while Marxist texts of the 1930s engage those of nationalism. On the other hand, we also find combinations of the two ideologies at play in each of the two cultural movements under consideration. We will discover the influence of socialism in the Harlem Renaissance and nationalism in the proletarian literary movement. Marxism and nationalism, in short, belong to an overriding and complex political dialogic of the modern period.

This book is divided into two parts. Part 1, "Nationalism in the Harlem

Renaissance," centers on the principle of ethnic nationalism that underwrote World War I, the peace settlement, and the Harlem Renaissance. In individual chapters, I address 1) the postwar movements of and highly-charged debates about black nationalism, socialism, and Americanism in the United States; 2) Alain Locke's *New Negro* anthology, which masterfully intervenes in these debates by defining the New Negro in solely nationalistic terms; and 3) the complex ways in which literature of the Harlem Renaissance participates in the dominant nationalistic rhetoric of the period. The triumph of postwar nationalism is encoded in many ways, from overt calls for a black nation, to the trope of national "awakening," to the recuperation of folk traditions and an immemorial past. Characteristic of ethnic-nationalist discourses, a number of black American postwar texts assert the existence of an innate racial quality in those of African ancestry and represent the New Negro as the culmination of a long historical process of coming to consciousness of a special destiny. Even the decision to create racial/national narratives—a practice dating back to the eighteenth century—receives a fresh impetus from the emergence of so-called new nationalities with the breakup of the great prewar empires after the war. I contend that the constructions of national identity by these black writers are both the products and reproducers of modern nationalism. As Timothy Brennan argues, "Nations . . . are imaginary constructs that depend for their existence on an apparatus of cultural fictions in which imaginative literature plays a decisive role" (49). Indeed, many texts from the Harlem Renaissance continue to "nationalize" their readers by presenting race pride and Americanism as the natural and therefore primary way to identify oneself and one's loyalties.

Part 2, "Internationalism and African American Writing in the 1930s," focuses on the political shift of black writers to the Communist Left during the Great Depression. Specifically, I analyze 1) the Communists' position on the "Negro Question" as it relates to discourses of nationalism and anti-imperialism that inform the production of proletarian literature and theory; 2) the radical poetry of Langston Hughes, which contains one of the strongest political critiques of postwar nationalism; and 3) the writings of Richard Wright, whose Marxist-psychoanalytic depictions of the psychological appeal of nationalism are still unparalleled in literature on nationalism. Black Communist literature discloses the ways in which capitalism produces working-class identities and interests that transgress politically constructed and divisive national and racial boundaries. Their internationalist writings are "inter" precisely because they maintain that the globalization of capitalism, particularly its standardization of an exploitative mode of production, creates the conditions for an international fraternity of the world's working classes. Part 2 provides in large part an immanent critique of nationalism, rooted in the incisive arguments of black Communist writers. I also draw, however, from a wide-range of contemporary studies of nationalism to further the historically limited critiques of the black internationalists who, ultimately, were likewise influenced by nationalism. With the kind of hindsight that the history and theory of nationalism now provides, the chief goal of part 2 is to highlight and to develop the strongest elements of the black Marxists' critiques of black nationalism.

By way of conclusion, the afterword, "Beyond Twentieth-Century Nationalisms in the Study of African American Culture," discusses some of the historical reasons for the nationalist limitations of current scholarship on black American culture. It also elaborates on the significance of this study's non-nationalist reconceptualization of interwar African American literature to future studies of black culture.

Understandably, some readers may wonder about the justifications for a study that goes against the grain of so much scholarship quite comfortable with the nationalist dimensions of interwar African American literature and especially of the Harlem Renaissance. Why the desire to move literature and literary scholarship beyond twentieth-century nationalisms? The long answer will be found in the detailed analyses of the politics and literature of the period. Here, I can only provide a short answer that touches upon some of the assumptions that inform this study of nationalism, Marxism, and black American literature.

My critique of nationalism concurs with the findings of numerous contemporary studies that historicize the concept, and thus denaturalize the ideology. Beginning in the nineteenth century, the criteria for establishing nationhood has been a vexed issue; nationalists have variously claimed that a group's possession of a common language, territory, race, ethnicity, religion, and/or psychology constitute nationhood, and only in the twentieth century does the ethnic-linguistic criterion of nationhood come to prevail. Regardless of how nationalists have defined nations, nationalism consistently maintains that each culture deserves its own state. As Ernest

Gellner plainly states, "Nationalism is a political principle which maintains that similarity of culture is the basic social bond. Whatever principles of authority may exist between people depend for their legitimacy on the fact that the members of the group concerned are of the same culture (or, in nationalist idiom, of the same 'nation')" (3–4). Thus, nationalism not only differentiates people primarily according to their "national" cultures but, just as importantly, by their loyalties to nation-states, real or imagined. After World War I, nationalist ideology was expressed in the much-touted phrase that nations have "the right to self-determination."

One of the problems with the principle of nationalism centers on the issues of culture and state. Are cultures homogenous, and do they provide a legitimate basis for social organization, centralized by a state? As Benedict Anderson argues, nations are "imagined communities," since "the members of even the smallest nation will never know most of their fellow-members, meet them, or even hear of them, yet in the minds of each lives the image of their communion" (15). Clearly, masses of people living within the political borders of a state are heterogeneous in terms of their class positions and occupations, educations, gender identities, political ideas, and so forth. Moreover, as the twentieth century progressed and the rivers of migrant laborers flowed into higher-paying labor pools, cultural heterogeneity only increased, which incensed many nationalists who wanted to preserve the "ethnic" purity of the nation. At the same time, the internationalization of capitalism, to cite an astoundingly "prophetic" document now over 150 years old, "compels all nations, on pain of extinction, to adopt the bourgeois mode of production" (Marx 488), the latter which erodes "pure" cultural difference. In short, the beloved common culture of nationalism is a myth, which is not to say that cultural differences do not exist, but only that they are not definitive of individuals in a capitalist world that is contradictorily fragmented in some ways and unified in others, and whose states have historically been the servants of class interests. Drawing the lines of the nation-state has been a historically contested practice, at times resulting in the false solution of what we now call "ethnic cleansing"—that is, genocide. While nationalism proper—the desire for a separate nation-state—is not a major issue for most black writers in the interwar period, the desire to establish a black national identity and culture that coexists, however tenuously, with an American identity and culture, is of crucial importance. Interwar black cultural nationalists, therefore, often refer to themselves as members of two national communities, the one of their birth and residence (as "Americans"), as well as the one of their ancestry and specific cultural traditions (as "Africans"). W. E. B. Du Bois's concept of "double consciousness," itself indebted to nineteenth-century theories of race and nation, is one instance of the kind of twin nationalism found in much African American literature and theory (*Souls* 38).

Another premise of this work is that nationalism has functioned as an ideology of class rule. Granted, one could argue as has Jurgen Habermas that in its early stages in the nineteenth century, nationalism played a vital role in creating the legal and psychological justification for the development of bourgeois republics, since "there would have been no driving force for such a transformation [from royal sovereignty to popular sovereignty] . . . if a nation of self-conscious citizens had not been emerging from the people of subjects" (285). Nonetheless, with the gradual consolidation of bourgeois state power over the decades and its abandonment of, or rather, difficulty in, maintaining its democratic justification, it became clear that the state's nationalist appeals to its citizenry in times of economic and political crises were ways of safeguarding or advancing its rule by shoring up support for its policies. One of the main reasons "foreign" wars continue to be potentially dangerous for state legitimacy is that the state's nationalist veneer wears thin as the body counts rise for the working-class "sons" of the respective "fatherlands." It is no wonder that imperialist states have found it in their long-term interests to fund, train, and militarily support "freedom fighters" of the occupied countries, when possible, to do the most dangerous and deadly work of ground war.

Nevertheless, in spite of its theoretical weaknesses and political uses, nationalism has had a brilliant, if still a historically short, career since the nineteenth century, precisely because it is one of those deceptive ideologies that work "with flatteringly and corruptly aroused hope" (Bloch 5). The greatest utopian appeal and mystification of nationalism has been its vision of the national community or, to use Marcus Garvey's metaphor, a "Bigger Brotherhood." Nationalists promise that the "free" national community of shared interests will somehow miraculously overcome the class divisions and conflicts endemic to capitalism without abolishing the structural inequalities of the capitalist mode of production. Its promise of a happy community, founded on a rich cultural and spiritual tradition, speaks to the great sense of alienation and disenfranchisement that people experience in a society fragmented by racism and class inequality. Whether the kind articulated by black nationalists, American nationalists, or inter-nationalists, nationalism promises power for the powerless, roots for the rootless, and inclusion for the excluded—certainly a difficult offer to reject. In the historical context of slavery and racism in the United States, black scholars and writers have found common cause with such an ideology that promises these rewards; to be sure, nationalism has appeared to many as the best way to defeat racism.

It is also important to bear in mind that the seeming permanence and naturalness of nationalism in the modern period has insidious political origins. Ruling classes of modern capitalist states have consistently used nationalism as their primary ideological weapon to quell the socialists' appeals for international solidarity among the working class and to discredit socialist visions of an egalitarian world without national borders. As Eric Hobsbawm notes, common to all nationalisms of the early twentieth century was their "rejection of the new proletarian socialist movements, not only because they were proletarian but also because they were, consciously and militantly *internationalist*, or at the very least non-nationalist" (*Nations and Nationalism* 122–23). Nationalism and internationalism came to function as two antagonistic ideologies, wherein "the advance of one [can be viewed] as equivalent to the retreat of the other" (123). Although it may be difficult to comprehend today, after the failures of twentieth-century socialist revolutions, socialism did and arguably still does provide the sharpest ideological challenge to the reign of capital and its inherent problems, such as exploitation, periodical crises, and war.

Consequently, capitalist ruling classes have historically waged a relentless campaign against socialism. The decisive moment during the last century when bourgeois nationalism became the bitter opponent of internationalism was the victory of the Russian Bolsheviks in 1917, which resurrected on a grand scale the long-feared specter of socialism for the imperial powers. One should pinpoint the beginning of the Cold War here since the policies of major capitalist powers became increasingly concerned with defeating the inroads of internationalism by appeals to nationalism. Herbert Hoover, then head of American relief in Europe, wrote in 1921: "The whole American policy during the liquidation of the Armistice was to contribute everything it could to prevent Europe from going Bolshevik or being overrun by their armies" (qtd. in Dutt 47). As we know, in the United States the nationalist bent of anticommunism was legitimated and enforced by the infamous Cold War institution, self-designated the House Un-American Activities Committee. The U.S. government knew who its enemies were, and they were precisely those making the most uncompromising demands for social equality in the United States, those calling for interracial working-class unity and the end to capitalism.

Anticommunism has clearly had a major impact on scholars of black culture, who too often replicate the very stereotypical arguments of Hoover, Attorney General Mitchell Palmer, Senator Joseph McCarthy, and other U.S. political figures who made it their life's work to banish the "spectre of communism" from the United States. Like their predecessors, many scholars of African American culture believe that if blacks were communists, then they simply must have been duped by left-wing political parties that did not have their best interests in mind. Apparently, for these scholars, to be black and communist is a more "curious thing" than to "make a poet black, and bid him sing!" In short, nationalism has been one of the greatest deterrents to considering rationally the analyses and ideals of the internationalists, which is an important reason that the minority voices of the black socialist writers discussed in this book deserve a greater hearing than they have had.

A non-nationalist approach to black cultural studies is already belated. As early as 1848 Marx foresaw that the laws of capitalist development would result in what today's liberal and conservative political economists are only now discovering: "globalization." Advanced capitalism is making national economies and cultures more and more redundant daily: at best, to modify an old Bolshevik slogan, society and culture are national in form (or name) but international in content. In other words, the internationalization of capitalism, which has been going on since its inception, is the precondition of this critique of nationalism and nationalist trends in black American literature and scholarship. Nonetheless, that much scholarship of black American literature remains entrenched in nationalist discourses necessitates that this critique be carried out sooner rather than even later. It is my hope that this book will contribute to the small but growing critical discussion of the nationalist paradigms that have shaped black cultural studies for decades, as well as to a reconsideration of the black literary and political Left who still have much to teach us about literature, the world, and ourselves.

Regarding my usage of racial and nationalistic concepts: the difficulties of imagining a true nation are equal to the difficulties of imagining the absence of nations or even of thinking devoid of nationalist concepts. To remain intelligible, in this study I will refer to "American" literature, "black Americans," "African Americans," and so forth, even though I risk reifying literature, identities, and classes in nationalistic terms. Additionally, in order to avoid distracting the reader with excessive quotation marks to signify the politically constructed and problematic usage of the terms *race* and *nation*, I will only occasionally quote these terms to emphasize a point. The reader should consider the imprecise use of these concepts as a historical limitation at the present time.

Nationalism
in the
Harlem Renaissance

Black Nationalist Discourse
in the Postwar Period

The war of 1914–1918 has created a new sentiment throughout the world. Once upon a time weaker peoples were afraid of expressing themselves, of giving vent to their feelings, but today no oppressed race or nation is afraid of speaking out in the cause of liberty. Egypt has spoken, Ireland has spoken, Poland has spoken and Poland is free, Egypt is free, Ireland is also free. Africa is now speaking.

Marcus Garvey, "A Solution for World Peace"

Nationalist, like racial and religious conflicts cut, [sic] across class lines and confuse the vision of the workers, making them susceptible to the intrigues and cunning of insincere and unscrupulous demagogues.

A. Philip Randolph, "Black Zionism"

Like other wars of the twentieth century, the exigencies of World War I unleashed a torrent of nationalism around the world. By the end of the war ethnic nationalism had triumphed as a principle ideology by which people conceived of their social identity (Hobsbawm, *Nations and National-ism* 130). President Woodrow Wilson, especially in the "Fourteen Points" speech he addressed to the U.S. Congress in 1918, was particularly instru-mental in devising the type of nationalism that would affect the peace settlement, lead to the formation of the League of Nations, and inspire many oppressed peoples with hopes of freedom. For Wilson, nationality and national sovereignty were founded on an ethnic-linguistic criterion: people of the same race and who spoke the same language constituted (in theory) a nation and had the right to self-determination. The ethnic-linguistic criterion of nationhood informs Point 12 of his Fourteen Points, for instance, wherein he asserts that the "Turkish portions of the present Ottoman Empire should be assured a secure sovereignty, but the other nationalities which are now under the Turkish rule should be assured an . . . absolutely unmolested opportunity of autonomous development" (Henig 76). The impact of Wilsonian nationalism on political struggles of the period cannot be underestimated. Indeed, the break up of the great multinational Romanov, Hapsburg, and Ottoman empires after the war fueled nationalist struggles around the world. "Given the official commitment of the victorious powers to Wilsonian nationalism," Eric Hobsbawm writes, "it was natural that anyone claiming to speak in the name of some oppressed or unrecognized people . . . should do so in terms of the national principle, and especially the right to self-determination" (136).

It is no wonder that a good number of black American intellectuals took up the banner of nationalism as a way of restating their case against racism and for equal rights in the United States and abroad. The spectrum of adaptations and elaborations of postwar nationalism to the specifics of black oppression is wide, but virtually every black intellectual speaks in nationalistic terms. Whereas during the Enlightenment, as Henry Louis Gates argues, reason and literacy signified humanity (1581), in the 1920s "nationness" becomes the sign of being human and entitlement to the social rights proclaimed by the bourgeois-democratic revolutions of the eighteenth and nineteenth centuries. In other words, nationalism is not just another political rhetoric of the times; rather, it constitutes the fundamental philosophical assumption about human identity and human value: a person without a nation, a person "dispossessed" and "disenfranchised," is really not a person at all. The sign of the nation—as the modern sign of human value and worth—is found in virtually every political position under consideration; it is ubiquitous—the trope with countless uses, equally serviceable for the purposes of the Ku Klux Klan, the U.S. government, or the Communist Party. Nationalism is the point beyond which interwar intellectuals and writers do not traverse, at least for any length of time, as if one would be hopelessly lost and alone in an unfamiliar terrain of thought.

The primary aim of this chapter is to examine the ideological effects of the postwar nationalist atmosphere on Marcus Garvey and W. E. B. Du Bois, the two figures who exerted the greatest influence on writers of the Harlem Renaissance. The chapter establishes some of the pervasive tropes, themes, and assumptions of nationalism and, more specifically, analyzes the ways in which these two writers adapt postwar nationalism to their own circumstances and political goals. It also demonstrates the ways in which Garvey and Du Bois, as nationalists, must be read in relation to their socialist counterparts, especially A. Philip Randolph and Chandler Owen, whose critiques of nationalism were the most uncompromising for a time on the spectrum of the American Left. This chapter lays the groundwork for my argument, developed in subsequent chapters, that writings from the Harlem Renaissance are woven tightly into the fabric of the larger nationalist discourse of the period that is, at the same time, defined against socialist conceptions of identity, social relations, and black liberation.

It has become a truism that nationalists are preoccupied with origins and traditions. To be sure, a "historical sense" is indispensable to anyone claiming any sort of nationalist identity and legitimization, and, as the timely T. S. Eliot once proclaimed, it is also "nearly indispensable to anyone who would continue to be a poet beyond his twenty-fifth year" ("Tradition and the Individual Talent" 449). The more heroic and glorious the founding of the nation, the greater the claims nationalists (and poets) can make for their intrinsic worth and rights. Consequently, common to nationalist projects is the labor of academics and intellectuals to create a collective memory that functions to produce a sense of destiny (Hroch 79). It is important to note, however, that the personages and events that form the collective memory are torn from a history and political circumstances far removed from those of the modern nationalists and renarrativized. As Benedict Anderson states, "It is the magic of nationalism to turn chance into destiny" (19).

Significantly, the rhetoric of national origins and traditions is inextricable from the rhetoric of family origins. Nationalists claim to have historical "fathers" and "mothers" whom they, like jealous children, defend against slander. The Founding Fathers are usually beyond reproach for the patriot, and Sigmund Freud appears to be right when in passing he notes a similarity between the way an adult can idealize his childhood and the way the "memories" of national origins were "compiled later and for

tendentious reasons" ("Leonardo" 456). The repression of socially unac-
ceptable desires and conflicts is mirrored at the political level: nationalists
represent the earliest days of the nation as an innocent time of greatness,
guided by the all wise and flawless patriarchs who deserve undying honor
and respect. Like the figures carved on Mount Rushmore, the Founding
Fathers loom larger than life. In so many ways, the goal of the nationalists
is to make it easy to "look up" to one's political parents and to obey their
wishes, which usually amount to the "tendentious reasons" or political
interests of the nationalist movement, whether they are to fight in a war
or a revolution.

The modern rhetoric of patrilineal national origins and identity is intertwined with a slightly older, pseudo-scientific racial discourse dating
back to the nineteenth century. Race and nation are interchangeable concepts for modern nationalists, resulting in what is properly known as
ethnic nationalism. The late nineteenth-century ethnic nationalism that tri-
umphs after the war—which is manifested in the Wilsonian attempt to
redesign national boundaries according to the ethnic or racial composition of the peoples concerned—functioned to strengthen the purported
patrilineal ties of the nation. "The symbolic kernel of the idea of
race . . . ," writes Etienne Balibar, "is the schema of genealogy, that
is, quite simply the idea that the filiation of individuals transmits from
generation to generation a substance both biological and spiritual and
thereby inscribes them in a temporal community known as 'kinship'"
(100). The concept of genetic heredity is foundational for the establishment of historical continuity and community of the nation or emergent
national group. For nationalists, the ties to one's political parents are as
"thick as blood," and, theoretically, as indisputable. Henceforth, "blood"
is a central trope, or, rather, the concept functions metonymically, signifying one's national origins and identity.

In the writings of Garvey and Du Bois, we find the rhetoric of special
racial origins, historical destiny, and filial ties typical of ethnic nationalism
in force. Of the two, Garvey offers the unadulterated Wilsonian or ethnic
nationalist vision, proposing that people of the African Diaspora return
"back" to Africa to found a black republic ruled by none other than himself. He rhetorically presents his nation-building program as a great family reunion: those of a "common family stock" ("Africa for the Africans"
1:52), temporarily separated at birth and in a sort of exile in Western

countries, will one day return to their true African "home." Rallying his cause at Madison Square Garden in 1924, he thus pleads, "Help us to gradually go home, America" ("Speech Delivered" 2:121), as if one could return to a place one had never set foot and call it home. The myth of African "blood relations" makes possible Garvey's entire notion of return. Indeed, the Garveyites' "Back to Africa" slogan contains a Dickensian logic: the orphaned children of the Diaspora discover their true bloodline and return home to reclaim their patrimony. It follows that the greatest threat to the "sons of Afric" is miscegenation, which is why Garvey equates it with "race suicide" in his statement of beliefs from 1924 ("What We Believe" 1:81). Like the myth William Faulkner explores in his literary works on declining southern aristocratic families, Garvey's concept of racial purity is requisite to a people's stability and good name.

At the center of the familial rhetoric lies the figurehead of the idealized mother—"Mother Africa." Garvey represents the African continent as the ur-mother, the origin of origins, whose particularly fertile body produced "the first great civilization of the world," while "the people of other races were groping in savagery, darkness and continental barbarism" ("History of the Negro" 2:82). "Motherland Africa" demands the deepest filial ties unaffected by the mock nationality that her offspring may possess due to "accident" of birth ("Africa for the Africans" 1:52). Garvey uses his concept of an essential black national identity and loyalty to "Mother Africa" to critique the ways in which European and American nationalism simultaneously builds and conceals the position of ruling classes. He writes,

> But we of the U.N.I.A. [Universal Negro Improvement Association] have studied seriously this question of nationality among Negroes—this American nationality, this British nationality, this French, Italian or Spanish nationality, and have discovered that it counts for naught when that nationality comes in conflict with the racial idealism of the group that rules. When our interests clash with those of the ruling faction, then we find that we have absolutely no rights . . . but in time of trouble they make us all partners . . . Hundreds of thousands—nay, millions of black men, lie buried under the ground due to that old-time camouflage of saving the nation. ("The Principles" 2:96)

Taken on its own, this quote exposes the myth and destructiveness of nationalism; yet, Garvey simply uses one nationalism (African) to critique another nationalism (non-African)—"that old-time camouflage"—and thus ignores the contradicting fact that the racism of the ruling factions during the war did not stop them from sacrificing their own working-class "sons" in hopes of garnering strategic political position and economic profit.

Not surprisingly, the sons of the motherland have the greatest role to play in the family-nation. As Wilson Moses points out, Garvey was a classical nationalist whose mission to "redeem" Africa included the "civilizing" of backward tribes and the expulsion of colonialists (44). "Mother Africa," represented as prostrate or, as in U.N.I.A.'s anthem, "upon [her] knees" (575), relies on her "husband" to call forth her "sons" to do battle against the colonial invaders: "We shall march out in answer to the cry of our fathers, who cry out to us for the redemption of our own country, our motherland, Africa" ("The Principles" 2:100). Here we have a horrific invocation of colonialism cast in terms of a family drama. In short, for Garvey, the black nation is one large, patriarchal family that shows due respect to its elder parents and to Africa's sons, whose charge is the redemption and defense of the motherland. (Women also play an important but supportive role. One female contributor to Garvey's *Negro World* writes, the black woman "has heard the call for nationhood and is prepared to answer it" by nurturing and encouraging her sons and husband in building an African nation [Parham 8].) Garvey aptly defines the imagined community of nationalism as "the Bigger Brotherhood" ("The Principles" 95)—an ideologically useful image that with a stroke symbolically establishes a filial intimacy and shared political purpose between (as Garvey liked to quote) four hundred million people of African ancestry.

Interestingly, while Garvey believes that "Mother Africa" always had an inherent worth and beauty in the world, he was not averse to giving her a makeover to render her more attractive to her modern sons "accidentally" living in Harlem. At the first U.N.I.A. Convention in 1920, Garvey clarifies his "Back to Africa" program, stating that he does not intend for black Americans to leave for Africa yet, but only after it has been urbanized. Blacks will return to Africa once "we get a Lenox Avenue and a Seventh Avenue . . . We have to put up those big apartment houses and get the bell boys to say 'Going Up' before you get Negroes to leave Harlem." Only after railroads and institutions have been built can "the command . . . be given, 'Come home' to Lenox Avenue, to Seventh Avenue"

("Developing Africa" 559). Ironically, then, Garvey transforms Africa into an image of urban America, which eradicates the pure "African" cultural differences he otherwise attempts to defend, and suggests that he was perhaps responsive to some of his critics who said that Africa would be estranging to black Americans. Nevertheless, the desire for an African "mother" and "home" constitute the origin and end of Garvey's black nationalism, and it is this desire that Richard Wright later depicts as a self-defeating Oedipal logic for black working-class men seduced by nationalism.

Du Bois's nationalistic rhetoric, on the other hand, is more complicated than Garvey's, since he asserts the existence of a dual identity or "double consciousness" that is both African and American, and, consequently, he rejects black nationalism proper. Arguing against the notion that the NAACP or the Pan-African Congress are separatist (like the Garveyites), Du Bois bluntly states, for example, "we are Americans . . . there is nothing so indigenous, so completely 'made in America' as we. It is absurd to talk of a return to Africa" ("Africa, Colonialism, Zionism" 639). He founds his claim to being American, which, understandably, he cannot clearly define, upon the duration of time that Africans have inhabited America, as well as their "gifts" to America. In his early masterpiece, The Souls of Black Folk (1903), as well as throughout his writings, he claims that if one has labored to create a nation, one is inherently a part of it, even if unrecognized in law. While Du Bois staunchly defends the civil rights of blacks in the United States, he does not look back upon the origins of America as glorious or heroic, since those origins were obviously intertwined with slavery. Instead, he takes the practiced Abolitionist tack of pressing on the conscience of his readers by pointing out the contradictions between an ideology of democracy and equality and the practices of a Jim Crow society.

Nonetheless, his rhetoric resembles Garvey's when he writes on the racial origins and basis of modern black identity. In truth, like his rival, Du Bois uncritically accepted a number of the pseudo-scientific racial theories that helped to prop up the system of slavery and have justified black oppression in general. In his early essay "The Conservation of Races" (1897), Du Bois displays the influence of the eighteenth- and nineteenth-century founders of "scientific" racism, such as Johann-Friedrich Blumenbach, Thomas Huxley, and Friedrich Raetzel, when he avows that "eight distinctly differentiated races" exist in the world (Slavs, Teutons,

English, Romance nations, Negroes, Semites, Hindoos, and Mongolians) (231). When Du Bois writes in *The Souls of Black Folk* that the problem of the twentieth century is the problem of the color line, he primarily means that new, egalitarian relationships must be developed between the hypostatic "darker" and the "lighter" races (45). As Eric Sundquist writes, "Du Bois never quite discarded his own initial view that race had some biological basis, but he constantly refined his own definitions over time, arguing more and more that race must be understood primarily as a cultural and political product" (37). For Du Bois, as for Novalis, racial character— whether biological or politically determined—is destiny, since "[n]egro blood has a message for the world" (*Souls* 39) that, if heard, would allow the historic race to fulfill its racial destiny.

Moreover, his early work contains the seeds of his ethnic nationalist perspective that flowers after the war. In "The Conservation of Races" he conceives of African Americans as a protonation, yet unrealized and unified by a state, but capable of nationhood due to their "common blood and language" (230, 233). Current with what appeared to him as a progressive trend of thought, Du Bois thus tacitly concurs with late nineteenth-century European ethnic nationalist discourses that largely used race and nation synonymously (Hobsbawm, *Nations and Nationalism* 108). Thus, in the 1920s, Du Bois, as one of the advanced guard of ethnic nationalists, did not miss his moment to push his program for the gradual liberation of Africa once Wilsonian nationalism became the official justification for nation building. It is difficult to imagine the program and principles of his Second Pan-African Congress, held in Paris simultaneously with the Paris Peace Conference, predating the war. For Du Bois, the "Negro race" has the right of "complete self government" ("Manifesto of the Second Pan-African Congress" 8).

Du Bois also develops the ethnic nationalist theme of glorious racial origins and traditions. One of the crucial cultural nationalist texts he published in the 1920s is an essay entitled "What Is Civilization? Africa's Answer" (1925). Valorizing African history beyond compare, Du Bois writes that Africa has given three things to the world that "form the essence of African culture: Beginnings, the village unit, and Art in sculpture and music" (202). Concerning beginnings, he makes a number of claims about the superiority of Africa, whose origin is "far more tremendous in its ultimate significance than anything that has happened since"

(202). Like Garvey, he professes that more so than other groups, Africans advanced "from animal savagery toward primitive civilization" (203). He also claims a great patrimony for Africa, which he conceives as "the Father of mankind" (203), since Africa originated modern industry (through the invention of smelting iron), religion, mythic archetypes (including the prototypes of the Greek gods), culture, and government (in the village unit).

Du Bois likewise privileges an African *Gemeinschaft* (an organic community based on kinship) over the European *Gesellschaft* (a rationalized, mechanistic community). He conceives of the African village unit as a "singularly persistent and eternal thing," whose "beginning stretched back in time thousands and thousands of years; it gathered to itself traditions and customs springing almost from the birth of the world" (204). He values the village unit because it achieved far better what the modern nation-state attempts, namely the socialization of the individual that "did not submerge and kill individuality" (205). He continues: "When the nation attempts to socialize the modern man the result is often a soulless Leviathan" (205). For Du Bois, the ancient African village has great charm because it provides a model of an integrated, spiritual black community unplagued by the ills of capitalism ("no monopoly, no poverty, no prostitution"). What "limited privilege of the chief and head men" is of no concern to Du Bois since they offer in return public service (204).

And not only ancient Africa holds charm above all other civilizations and peoples for Du Bois. In "Little Portraits," he writes passionately of modern Africa:

> This is not a country, it is a world—a universe of itself and for itself, a thing Different, Immense, Menacing, Alluring. It is a great black bosom where the Spirit longs to die . . . Africa is the Spiritual Frontier of human kind . . . [There] will come a day—an old and ever, ever young day when there will spring in Africa a civilization without coal, without noise, where machinery will sing and never rush and roar, and where men will sleep and think and dance and lie prone before the rising suns, and women will be happy . . . We shall dream the day away and in cool dawns, in little swift hours, do all our work. (647)

Represented as a mildly industrial utopia, Du Bois's Africa is the alpha and omega of the ideal society—and even he cannot resist metaphorizing utopia as a return to a blissful childhood, secure at the mother's "great black bosom," and free from the cares of modern industrial capitalism and racism. He also represents Africa as a repository for bourgeois desire, a place where, as Countee Cullen speculates, "bronze" men and "regal black" women lounge and love ("Heritage" 250). Or, as Harry Taylor versifies in U.N.I.A.'s Negro World, Africa is an "Earthly paradise, / Everything that's nice, / Where a man's a man, / Richest thing in land" (6). To be sure, in the 1920s Du Bois and these writers were under the spell of ethnic nationalism. Thus, in the 1940s, after he had renounced ethnic nationalism and had become a Communist, Du Bois significantly revised his idyllic conception of Africa; "there is no 'Africa,'" he later writes; "There is in the continent of Africa no unity of physical characteristics, of cultural development, of historical experience, or of racial identity" ("The Realities in Africa" 656).

Du Bois and Garvey's similar idealizations of Africa and African history in the 1920s supply their respective organizations with prototypes for black national identity and politics in the 1920s. By relying on notions of genetic heredity and destiny, they assume that the racial or national greatness of ancient Africa proves that modern African Americans or Africans in America can build a new nation of equal greatness. In both cases, a "return" to Africa (whether physical or cultural) furnishes the figures of hope for future social greatness and racial/national self-sufficiency. Yet, it must also be said that the idealization of African history elides important issues of identity and politics, past and present. Needless to say, one could take issue with their inverse chauvinism, but, for our immediate purposes, it is enough to point out that we have here a mystification and gendering of origins that passes over troubling details about unegalitarian ancient social practices and values. Du Bois and Garvey, for instance, seem unbothered by the class and gender inequalities inherent to the village unit, whether we focus on the patriarchal or matriarchal social organization of early Africa. Moreover, G. Mokhtar points out in The General History of Africa, for example, a number of details that refute Du Bois's racial chauvinism, including the difficulty of ascribing race to Egyptians (15)—as if one can speak meaningfully about historical development and causality using the always reductive category of race. Additionally, notes Mokhtar, "the history of Africa, from −7000 to +700, still consists largely of suppositions" (2). Perhaps not surprisingly, the patriarchal privilege of the chief and headmen is a model for the male-dominant NAACP and U.N.I.A. African "socialization" has its male privileges.

Certainly, the black nationalists' nostalgia and goal for an "earthy paradise," modeled on an idealized familial structure of ancient African societies, expresses an important counterdesire to living under monopoly capitalism, where people experience a multileveled social fragmentation owing to deep class, racist, nationalist, and colonial divisions, as well as to the growth of huge and at times alienating urban centers. As Raymond Williams demonstrates in *The Country and the City*, a wide range of writers laboring under the great transformations wrought by capitalism in its successive phases register the European and American city as corrosive of smaller organic communities, the latter which, however, they swathe in a retrograde historical desire. In the African village, Du Bois discovers the realization of many desires unfulfilled under industrial and urban capitalism. Africa seems to provide social intimacy, equality, compassion, and dignity not found in the soulless, unegalitarian, cold, alienated urban West—the "Leviathan." In the "Bigger Brotherhood," Garvey is surrounded by the love of a great big family united by blood, a shared history, and future prospects. Yet, ironically, "nationalism," writes Ernest Gellner, "is a phenomenon of *Gesellschaft* using the idiom of *Gemeinschaft*: a mobile anonymous society simulating a closed cozy community" (74). The *Gesellschaft* of capitalism produces the very desires for a "return" to the nationalist *Gemeinschaft*.

Just as importantly, Du Bois and Garvey's black nationalism expresses their desire to move from the colonial and segregated margins of modern history to the center of history. Indeed, Du Bois and Garvey's black individual, after being counted out of society and history by racist and colonial ideologies and practices, finds "himself" once again at the center of world history, and as a vanguard for all oppressed peoples. Nationalist myth shares the universalist desires of the contemporaneous modernist myth, which, as Terry Eagleton argues, "figure[s] as a return of the Romantic symbol, a reinvention of the Hegelian 'concrete universal,' in which every phenomenon is secretly inscribed by a universal law, and any time, place or identity pregnant with the burden of the cosmic whole . . . a history in crisis might once more be rendered stable and significant, reconstituted as a set of hierarchical planes and correspondences" (319). Du Bois and Garvey's myth claims that black identity is both particular (pluribus) and universal (unum). Africa is, proclaimed an U.N.I.A. banner, "a Nation One and Indivisible" ("Report of U.N.I.A. Parade" 493). The very name of Garvey's organization is a fine instance of the nationalist "concrete universal": the "universal Negro" has overcome his inferior status in a Western philosophical discourse and political practice; he has overcome simultaneously a damning particularism and a prohibited universalism; he has regained the center.

What may appear to us in retrospect as a false universalism, however, Garvey and Du Bois explain away through the concept of nationalist "awakening" or the "Awakener." "The dormission of nationalism, though not normally referred to by this name," Gellner explains, "is one of the absolutely central doctrines of nationalism" (Nationalism 9). If people of African descent have not consistently exhibited a common identity and purpose—embodied by the desire for a separate nation-state or at least black businesses, political organizations, and communities—then they must not have been awake to their "true" selves. Implicit in the notion of a nationalist awakening is the assumption that all people of African descent have an essential identity and purpose that, after being politically repressed and therefore forgotten by many, is being rediscovered so that the "race" may fulfill its destiny. The operative trope here is that of personification, without which the race or nation could not exist, let alone awaken.

In Garvey's writings, as well as in many of the contributions to the Negro World, we find explicit references to nationalist awakening. For example, Garvey claimed that U.N.I.A. "represents the hopes and aspirations of the awakened Negro" ("Speech Delivered" 2:118). Lelia V. Miller effectively writes on this theme in a poem published by the Negro World, aptly entitled "Wake Up, Sleeping Africa!":

I do not know why Africa lies slumbering,
Why all the dark world sleeps in such pathetic woe,
While on and up through recent centuries numbering
The white race marches upward to Life's goal.

Perhaps the sleep is only but the resting
From fame long past of glories that are dead;
Perhaps, some happy day, when ends the testing,
The darker world shall take her place ahead. (6)

The remaining stanzas are an exhortation to the black race to awaken and rise "as Garvey bids his race to conquer" (6). Like so many other members of U.N.I.A., Miller revered Garvey as the Awakener who will rouse "the darker world" from its slumber. Indeed, even Garvey cast himself in the role of a Moses who leads his people to the Promised Land.

The trope of awakening also figures prominently in Du Bois's writings, but he uses it interchangeably to rouse black and American national identities, as the political situation required. He calls on America to awaken, for instance, to its democratic ideals on the eve of its entry to the war, to fight to make America free from racism: "Awake! Put on they [sic] strength, America—put on thy beautiful robes. Become not a bye word and jest among the nations by the hypocrisy of your word and contradiction of your deeds" ("Awake America" 379). He sounds the black nationalist note of awakening when he urges black Americans to greater self-determination. In a section of one of his editorials from 1918, entitled "Awake, Put on Thy Strength, O Zion," he urges African Americans to support black universities "for the day of passing the hat for Negro education is nearing a close" (114). Understandably, Du Bois's unstinting campaign to promote black businesses, leaders, schools, and racial pride made him into a figure of the black Awakener for many African Americans. (A noteworthy example for this study is Langston Hughes's inscription of "The Negro Speaks of Rivers" (1921) to Du Bois, since the poem is a meditation on the kind of racial awakening urged by Du Bois). That Du Bois counted himself among one of the "Talented Tenth" who must play the role of Awakener and leader goes without saying; however, unlike Garvey, he was not one to flatter himself with the appellations (or dress!) of heroic historical personages.

As suggested in the introduction, nationalism and internationalism generally confronted each other as antagonistic ideologies in the postwar period. The nationalism of Du Bois, Garvey, and the Harlem Renaissance cannot be fully understood except within this political dynamic and context. Indeed, the rhetoric of nationalism is historically motivated by a desire to foreclose the political possibilities opened up by the Bolshevik Revolution. We find running dialogues in the pages of the *Negro World* and the *Crisis* with the three varieties of socialism current in the period, namely those of the Socialist Party (SP), the African Blood Brotherhood (ABB), and the Communists' Workers Party (WP). This may seem an odd fact, since, in spite of the victory of the Bolsheviks in Russia, internationalism did not gain a strong foothold in the black American literary and intellectual scene during the 1920s. A number of convincing arguments have been advanced by historians of the American Left, such as Philip S. Foner and Theodore Kornweibel, for the slow growth of socialism after the war. Certainly the success of the U.S. government's crackdown on left-wing organizations during and after the war (particularly through the "Palmer Raids"), as well as the weakness of the American Left to address adequately the specific issues that faced black workers, did not help its cause. Yet the agitation the socialists did muster, along with the world-historical event of the Bolshevik Revolution covered by the press, albeit unsympathetically, exercised a significant challenge to and pressure on the rhetoric of the nationalists.

The socialists' greatest challenge to Du Bois and Garvey is their conception of identity as a more complicated affair than ethnic nationalism makes out. While great ideological differences existed between the SP, ABB, and the WP, they were in agreement that under a global capitalist system of production and political rule, workers, irrespective of race or nation, have significant class experiences in common that shape their identity and should shape their politics and cultural production. They also believed that the liberation of black Americans could only ultimately be achieved by allying with white workers to overthrow capitalist rule and to establish a dictatorship of the multiracial proletariat, a workers' democracy.

The black Socialists, at least up until 1924, were the most critical of wartime and postwar nationalism, especially of Garveyism. As early as 1919, the Socialist editors of the Messenger, A. Philip Randolph and Chandler Owen, published scathing critiques of the principle of nationality that underwrote the peace treaty and the formation of the League of Nations, the latter which they saw as a means of the ruling classes "to put down a recalcitrant, rising working class" ("The Peace Treaty" 5). In the March 1919 issue of the Messenger, they published a one-page credo entitled "The New Patriotism" that argues against the "old" patriotisms of nation-states. "The new patriotism," they write, "is color-blind, flag-blind, Kaiser-blind," since it rejects national categories and looks into the "substance" of politics; discounting the epiduralization of humanity (to use Frantz Fanon's term), the "new patriotism" discovers that all people "look alike," and thus rejects ethnic nationalist chauvinism. Viewing nations as social constructs, they also state that "[t]he new patriotism cannot hate a man because he is born or lives on the other side of a strip of water or an imaginary line" (26).

Roughly three years later, Randolph works out the tenets of "The New Patriotism" more fully in three pieces entitled "Garveyism" (1921), "Black Zionism" (1922), and "The Only Way to Redeem Africa" (1922–1923). In "Garveyism," Randolph, critical of the world tour of the post-war nationalist bandwagon, argues that Garvey's rhetoric replicates the national chauvinism of the Great War, which used as its "psychological armor and spear" such slogans as "Britania, Britania rules the waves, Briton will ne'r be slaves," "self determination of smaller nationalities," "100 per cent Americanism," "Deutschland Uber Alles," "Pan-Slavism," and so forth (248). Garveyism operates according to "the doctrine of similarity": it mimics the ideology and form of the dominant imperialists.

In "Black Zionism," Randolph takes issue with the method (not the objective) of nationalists or "Zionists." He slights the political methods of Zionists (namely, the founding of a Jewish, Irish, or black state), which he perceives as inconsistent with their stated objectives (the liberation of an entire people). Jewish Zionism, Randolph writes, "can not solve the problems of the Jewish workers. Under a Jewish State, the same class divisions would reappear that manifest themselves between the Jewish employees and employers in the Western European and American countries. In very truth, *wherever the private ownership in the social tools and sources of wealth production and exchange is sanctioned, the irrepressible and irreconcilable conflict, will appear*" (331, emphasis added). The endemic conflict of class interests under capitalism destroys the possibility of founding a homogenous, cooperative, and peaceful national community. Randolph only cedes a limited value to the "march of nationalism" in cases where it arises in opposition to foreign rule and exposes the "class despotism" inherent to the capitalist economic system.

In "The Only Way to Redeem Africa," Randolph attacks Garveyism as quixotic (Nov. 1922, 522). Randolph's measure of a political program is whether or not it could truly provide egalitarian social relations at central sites of power. In the January 1923 installment of the article, he writes, "*Black despotism is as objectionable as white despotism. A black landlord is no more* sympathetic with black tenants than white landlords are. A Negro is no more interested in having his pocketbook stolen by a black thief than he is in having it stolen by a white thief. Death is no sweeter at the hands of a black murderer than it is at the hands of a white murderer" (569). Black nationalism is utopian in the sense that it claims it can abolish the evils of capitalism—such as unemployment, exploitation, inequality—by restaffing capitalism with a black bourgeoisie that would treat its like-colored workers with fairness. Hence, "by making the question of unemployment an issue as between white and black men," Garvey misses the fact that unemployment "is a product of the capitalist system which brings about overproduction at certain cycles, and consequent unemployment of workers regardless of race, creed, nationality or color" ("Garveyism" 251). For the black Socialists, unemployment and exploitation are first and foremost class problems intrinsic to the capitalist mode of production.

In "The Only Way" Randolph also criticizes Garvey's conceptual homogenization of Africa and African identity. He makes the rather obvious points that "Africa is a continent, not a nation"; it comprises an area of 11,500,000 square miles; and it is composed of "several nations that are as distinct, separate and different in customs, traditions, manners, culture, language, race and religion as are the nations of Europe" (Nov. 1922, 534). Randolph suggests that Garvey misuses and reifies the concept of "nation," since he substitutes the concept of continent (a formation of nature) with the concept of nation ("an artificial product of man"). Garvey reduces the heterogeneity of an entire continent into that of the mythic homogeneity of a nation. In short, as Randolph adds in the following installment, Garveyism, like other nationalisms, is "a 100 per cent fetishism," but a fetishism that works to an extent since the social origins of the fetish are concealed by the geographical distance of and misinformation surrounding Africa (Dec. 1922, 541). With biting sarcasm, Randolph concludes his critique of Garvey:

> To him there is a racial and nationality homogeneity in Africa: all tribes possessing one mind, awaiting the time, when, according to the Garveyites, Brother Marcus will pull the Houdini stunt and touch a cable button from his imperial dais in "Slavery Hole" (misnamed "Liberty Hall") on 138th Street, New York City, and instantaneously, through his magic power, millions of African Legionaires will spring forth out of the region of nothingness and pass thousands of miles through thin air, land upon Africa and, presto! all of the armed forces of Great Britain, France, Portugal and Spain will get scared and skiddo. (Nov. 1922, 524)

And Randolph was not alone in his critical assessment of Garvey's simplistic view of Africa and African liberation. To be sure, neither could the socialist poet Claude McKay, although in other ways sympathetic to Garvey, restrain himself from commenting that Garvey "talks of Africa as if it were a little island in the Caribbean Sea. Ignoring all geographical and political divisions, he gives his followers the idea that this vast continent of diverse tribes consists of a large homogenous nation of natives struggling for freedom and waiting for Western Negroes to come and help them drive out the European exploiters" ("Garvey as a Negro Moses" 68). For the black Socialists, Garveyism represents nothing less than an elaborate magic trick to foster an incapacitating divisiveness between the working classes and to lead black workers away from socialism ("Black Zionism" 335). As James Oneal, a white leader of the SP, wrote in the "The Next Emancipation" (serialized in the *Messenger*): "Masters will use the color line, or religion, or differences of nationality, to divide workers" (June 1922, 421). Contrary to Garveyism, then, the Socialists' implied "bigger brotherhood" extends to all workers but significantly excludes the bourgeoisie because of basic conflicts of class interest. It is no wonder that for Attorney General A. Mitchell Palmer, who conducted infamous postwar raids against left-wing organizations, the *Messenger* was "by all odds the most able and the most dangerous of all the negro publications" (qtd. in Kornweibel 91).

The black Socialists, of course, had their failings. The editors of the *Messenger* turned a blind eye, for instance, to the theoretical and political weaknesses of the SP on questions concerning the special forms of oppression faced by black workers. As Philip S. Foner notes, the SP only published one pamphlet on the "Negro Question" between 1919 and 1935, namely that of Oneal, which in itself did not go beyond the traditional SP view that black workers do not suffer super-exploitation or extra-oppression due to racism (320). The *Messenger* editors also tacitly sided with the right wing of the SP split of 1919. That is to say, they sided with those in the SP who believed that the Bolshevik Revolution could not be duplicated in the United States and that, to the contrary, the war had strengthened capitalism, making immediate revolution nearly impossible (303). The consequence of such a position led the Socialists to concentrate their struggles on creating reform, not revolution, even though they believed that only a socialist revolution could eventually end social inequality. In other words, they worked in practice to strengthen the reformist and ultimately idealist politics of the labor movement that settled for minor concessions that could be taken away by the capitalist class and its legal representatives as long as the working class did not have power. Their reformism finally leads them into an openly anticommunist position and a capitulation to purely reformist politics. Thus, in a 1923 editorial, "The Menace of Negro Communists," Owen and Randolph ridicule the Communist Third International, the Workers Party (formed out of the left wing of the SP split), black Communists, and the notion of revolution. Nonetheless, the black Socialists' insistence in the early 1920s on viewing the "Negro Question" as a question of class shielded them from framing the oppression of blacks as a racial or national question, the latter a theoretical error that fostered a host of nationalistic myths about black identity and liberation that would dominate Left thinking until the 1960s.

Relative to those of the black Socialists, the arguments of the ABB and the WP were less antagonistic in principle to nationalism but still functioned to challenge the purely racial and nationalistic ideologies of Du Bois and Garvey. The ABB was a socialist-nationalist organization whose rhetoric partakes interchangeably of Wilsonian nationalism, Garveyism, and Bolshevism. In the "Program of the A.B.B." (1921), we find the nationalist metaphor of filiation at work when the ABB refers to Africa as "our motherland," thereby implicitly including itself as composed of Africa's "children" (16). Echoing Garvey, Theo. Burrell, a founding member of the ABB and a contributing editor to the organization's magazine, the *Crusader*, unhesitatingly writes that "[t]he time has come when the sons of Africa should unite" in order to liberate Africa (6). The ABB's "Program" also proclaims that Africa can be free only when the African "become[s] the master of his own motherland" (16). Unlike the black Socialists, the ABB suggests that black identity is racial and that the liberation of Africa is also a national issue. At the basis of the ABB's ethnic nationalism are the pseudoscientific racial discourses of the late nineteenth and early twentieth centuries. Like Garvey and Du Bois, the ABB speaks about the blood of Africa that unites people of African descent; hence the name of the organization. "[I]n the veins of no human being," they write, "does there flow more generous blood than in our own; in the annals of the world, the history of no race is more resplendent with honest, worthy glory than that of the Negro race, members of which founded the first beginnings of civilization" ("A Race Catechism" 11). To be sure, the "blood brotherhood's" name could have easily been misconstrued at the time as referring to Garveyism.

However, the ABB also supported the Bolshevik Revolution and the Communist Third International, which put the organization to the left of the Garveyites and Du Bois. The "Program" affirms that the oppression of Africa is equally a class issue, one of imperialism, not simply of racism. The ABB therefore warns blacks not to "pledge loyalty to the flags of our murderers and oppressors" (18). On the contrary, it argues for an alliance with all oppressed workers, including class-conscious white workers. The ABB even views non-class-conscious white workers as potential allies, though they "have not yet realized that all workers regardless of race or color have a common interest" (18). In short, in the ABB's writings we find a tension between "Race Patriotism" or Pan Africanism ("A Race Catechism" 11) and a class-based socialist critique that views capitalism and imperialism as the root of the problem. Unlike the nonsocialist black nationalists, the ABB advocated the formation of multiracial unions as a strategy of fighting against capitalist exploitation and imperialist plunder.

Largely as a result of its own nationalist bent, the ABB expressed sympathy with Garveyism between 1919 and 1921. It had only publicly criticized Garvey's decision to elect "His Supreme Highness" and other leaders of the world's black populations in New York City (without international representation) and his refusal to lay open the questionable business accounts of his Black Star Line. But the ABB began to take a firm, principled stance against Garveyism after Garvey made clear his anticommunism by expelling the Brotherhood from U.N.I.A.'s Second International Negro Congress (1921) and after he demonstrated that his "race patriotism" and black nationalism found common cause with the Ku Klux Klan's own desire to deport African Americans "back to Africa." In a pointed attack against Garvey immediately following their expulsion from the Second Congress, the ABB's leadership published an article entitled "Garvey Shows His Hand," wherein they rhetorically ask:

> Is Mr. Garvey really in earnest when he talks about the liberation of Africa? . . . What does Mr. Garvey mean by pledging Negro loyalty to the United States Government and giving that government a blanket endorsement for all its future wars, whether those wars be against friendly Soviet

Russia, racial Japan, China, or Haiti; and whether the U.S. government takes steps to protect Negroes in their constitutional rights or refuse, as in the past, to take such steps? What does he mean by advising Negroes to "be loyal to all flags under which they live?" How can Negroes liberate Africa if they remain loyal to Great Britain, France, Belgium, and other European plunderers? (23)

It is clear that the ABB primarily takes issue here with the way Garvey's support of U.S. nationalism is in practice support for imperialism, racism, and segregation. In its "Program," which was also published in the same issue of the *Crusader* as the above article, the ABB's leadership makes it clear that, contra Garvey, it allies itself with the Communist Third International, precisely because the Third International is anti-imperialist (17). Taking another jab at Garvey, the leadership also writes that their "strength cannot be organized by vain indulgence in mock-heroics, empty phrases, unearned decorations or titles, and other tomfoolery" ("Program" 18). By 1921, for the ABB, Garvey had revealed himself to be a charlatan expert in bluffing his followers into believing his grand promises of black liberation while not having an actual, realizable program—a strong hand of cards.

The WP also presented a socialist challenge to nationalism, but, of the three left-wing parties of the period, it soft-pedaled black nationalism the longest. On the one hand, for most of the decade the WP upheld the SP's view of the "Negro Question," in spite of the former's split from the latter. Like the SP, the WP did not clearly differentiate between the specific interests and conditions of black and white workers. Hence, according to the "Program" of the WP's founding convention of 1921, "The Workers Party will support the Negroes in their struggle for liberation, and will help them in their fight for economic, political, and social equality. It will point out to them that the interests of the Negro workers are identical with those of the white" (qtd. in Foster 193). Or, similarly, skirting the issue of the super-exploitation and racist oppression of black workers, Communist Rose Pastor Stokes states in 1923: "Communists know no race or color differences, as they know no national boundary lines. Common oppression ultimately places all workers in one camp for the struggle against the oppressors" ("The Communist International and the Negro" 32). Unfortunately, not having yet freed itself from the predominantly white SP's focus on primarily organizing the white working class, the purported agents of an American proletarian revolution, the WP in practice did little to address the situation of black workers. As Philip S. Foner and James A. Allen note, "With such a general outlook, what was distinctive in the situation of Blacks was overlooked and their special needs and demands were ignored" (viii).

On the other hand, the WP expressed an ambivalent attitude toward Garvey's nationalism. Robin D. G. Kelley succinctly notes, as a member of the Communist International, the WP had "adopted a set of theses describing blacks as a nationality oppressed by world-wide imperialist exploitation" (*Race Rebels* 107). Consequently, in the early 1920s the WP had the "tendency to overlook, if not condemn, the national aspects of . . . [Garveyism], while welcoming its mass character" (Foner and Allen ix). Only in retrospect did the WP criticize its inclination "to look upon Garvey as a 'natural' leader of the American Negro masses and thereby unconsciously aid his work of confusion and betrayal" (qtd. in Dunne 104). More specifically, it was not until Garvey openly proclaimed at the Fourth International Convention of the U.N.I.A. (1924) a collaborationist attitude toward the Ku Klux Klan (whom he saw as representative of white Americans) that the WP began to end its courtship with U.N.I.A. And, even as late as 1926, we find Communists mourning the demise of U.N.I.A. when Robert Minor, head of the Party's Central Committee work on blacks, laments that since U.N.I.A. was composed primarily of black workers who were politically active after the war, "the destruction of such an organization of the Negro masses, under the circumstances, would be a calamity" (137). However, by the decade's close, and especially during the first half of 1930s, the Communists became some of the sharpest critics of Garveyism and led the most protracted and effective fights against racism and the extra-exploitation of black workers. In this sense, the Communists took up the work of the defunct ABB, which folded in 1923, and the black Socialists, who had abandoned their radical politics by the mid 1920s.

Knowing full well the sharp criticisms of nationalism from the Left, Garvey and Du Bois were often on the defensive. Their responses to the internationalists' class analyses of black Americans center on the question of identity. Garvey was particularly hostile to the socialists, since he conceived of identity in simplistic terms and was not eager to work with any

other organization that he did not control. For Garvey, the biological
determinist, races are inherently antagonistic to each other. In Social Dar-
winist terms, he maintains that the white race would never cede any of
its power or privilege to the black race. Fighting for civil rights in any
white nation was a waste of time for blacks, an "impossible dream . . .
that shall never materialize" and that distracted "the Negro from the real
solution and objective of securing nationalism" ("The Negro, Communism" 2:70–71). Garvey's implied syllogism runs: all whites want to oppress blacks; socialists are white; therefore, socialists want to oppress
blacks. Metaphorically, for Garvey, "there is no difference between two
roses looking alike, and smelling alike, even if some one calls them by
different names. Fundamentally what racial difference is there between a
white Communist, Republican or Democrat?" (69).

To say the least, such a rhetorical question displays willful ignorance,
since he knew that a white Communist such as Rose Pastor Stokes, whom
he let speak at the second annual U.N.I.A. Convention in 1921, differed
greatly in her view of the "Negro Question" than, say, President Warren
Harding, who claimed that "the colored man of the South has his only
opportunity by falling in the ranks behind the leadership of white men"
(qtd. in the *Messenger*, Nov. 1921, 275). Harding also advertised his ignorance in one of his preinaugural discussions with black leaders in Florida.
Eugene Trani and David Wilson write: "During a long rambling discourse
it became plain that he [Harding] had never heard of the Tuskegee Institute nor of its famous founder, Booker T. Washington" (192–93). Harding also made it plain during his administration that he was against
social equality, since he did not support the Dyer antilynching bill in
Congress or do anything to abolish segregation or to restrain the Ku Klux
Klan. In contrast to Harding's racist ignorance, Communist Rose Pastor
Stokes spoke in part to the U.N.I.A Convention:

> We must stand together as workers. We need not seek to place lines; or,
> I should say, on the contrary, if you prefer to draw lines, if you prefer to
> say: "Oh, we are black and you are white"; very well fellow-workers. But
> co-operation, in the interest of your own freedom, is as necessary in
> relation to the great revolutionary working-class struggle of the world as
> it is necessary for you to build your own powerful organization. ("The
> Cause of Freedom" 134)

Garvey's racial and, indeed, racist perspective thus made him ignore the political and class determinants of thinking and acting that help to differentiate political friends from enemies. Hence, any white person who proclaimed a desire for racial equality Garvey deemed a hypocrite, since he viewed race, not antiracist ideas or actions, as definitive of identity and true interests. Thus, he could claim that he "regard[s] the Klan, the Anglo-Saxon clubs and White American societies, as far as the Negro is concerned, as better friends of the race than all other groups of hypocritical whites put together" ("The Negro, Communism" 2:71).

Garvey's hostility to socialism was also motivated by his own bourgeois aspirations that necessarily depended upon the maintenance of the capitalist mode of production. He openly viewed capitalism as "necessary to the progress of the world" ("Capitalism and the State" 2:72). Therefore, his advocacy of state capitalism—where the state regulates the amount of capital individuals and corporations can accumulate and appropriates the surplus capital for national investment—was a petit bourgeois challenge not only to the big bourgeoisie's monopoly of markets but equally to the communists' critique of the inherent inequalities of capitalism and their vision of a classless society that exists outside or in place of the capitalist world economy. His nationalism functioned as a means for enlisting investors, workers, sympathizers, and propagandists for his various economic enterprises, from the Black Cross Navigation and Trading Company and the Negro Factories Corporation to the Black Star Line of steamships that would presumably one day transport the diasporic black masses to the African empire over which he would rule. And, of course, to rule Africa would in itself be extremely profitable because, as Randolph notes in "The Only Way to Redeem Africa," "it is the home of rubber, gold, diamonds, cocoa, kernels, iron, coal, etc.," a home plundered by Western imperialists precisely for its wealth (Feb. 1923, 614). In this respect, he did not significantly differ from other capitalist and imperialist ideologues of the modern period who used both nationalism and anticommunism as means of concealing their class interests.

Du Bois, to the contrary, expressed an ambivalent and contradictory relationship to socialism in the 1920s. In an editorial from the 1919 "Labor Number" of the Crisis, Du Bois appears cautiously optimistic about the Bolshevik Revolution. Arguing against "intellectual provincialism" among blacks, he states the need "to know the problems of other forward forging groups whose difficulties are inevitably intertwined with ours" ("Forward" 234), namely those of Ireland, India, and Russia. On Russia, he writes:

> the one new Idea of the World War—the idea which may well stand in future years as the one thing that made the slaughter worthwhile—is an Idea which we are like [sic] to fail to know because it is today hidden under the maledictions hurled at Bolshevism.
>
> It is not the murder, the anarchy, the hate, which for years under Czar and Revolution have drenched this weary land, but it is the vision of great dreamers that *only those who work shall vote and rule.* (234–35)

Du Bois's depth of understanding allows him to view the success of the Revolution in terms of its negation, Czarist Russia, referred to by progressive intellectuals of the time as "the prison house of peoples." His critical view is also borne out in a 1927 editorial, entitled "Judging Russia." In this piece, written after having visited the Soviet Union, he praises the accomplishment of the Revolution for its "dictatorship of the proletariat," yet questions whether or not it can be sustained. In response to attacks on the Soviet Union as a "dictatorship," Du Bois writes, "We are all subject to this form of government," albeit our dictatorship being that of the millionaire (190). What is more, on the issue of potential political corruption in the fledgling Soviet Union, Du Bois argues that "here Russia has no monopoly" (190). In "Judging Russia," the fundamental issue for Du Bois is whether or not a society can "make the worker and not the millionaire the center of modern power and culture . . . If you can, the Russian Revolution will sweep the world" (190).

Nevertheless, during the 1920s Du Bois kept his distance from the Socialists and Communists, even though he considered himself a socialist since he advocates a "social control of wealth" ("The Negro and Radical Thought" 103). It is in the context of the American Left that we see how his nationalist ideology determines his speculations on the black working class. For example, in 1921, he argues against the socialist notion that working-class blacks should join the class struggle against the bourgeoisie. He claims that racism among white workers prevents blacks from being a part of the white proletariat; the socialists' claim that black and white workers constitute a single proletariat with common interests is a myth ("Class Struggle" 151). Moreover, Du Bois argues that the numerically small black bourgeoisie came up from the ranks of the working class and are, therefore, sympathetic to the black working class (152). Given these two factors, he concludes that the "salvation" of blacks lies in developing their own bourgeoisie and finance capitalists—ultimately in the establishment of a national black bank—since their "more democratic organization and . . . widespread inter-class sympathy" will result in prosperity for all (152). In other words, he agrees with Garvey that a common racial identity, the foundation of black nationalist enterprise, has primacy over class identity and interests. The theme that white workers have more in common with their white bosses than with black workers (and vice versa) pervades Du Bois's arguments in the 1920s. The white worker voluntarily is a "co-worker [with white imperialists] in the miserable subjugation of over half the world" ("Socialism and the Negro" 247). Both Du Bois and Garvey express their well-founded skepticism concerning the racism of white workers, especially given the race riots and the exclusionary practices of the white-led unions in the 1920s. However, Garvey naturalizes white racism, whereas Du Bois believes that "interracial sympathy" would somehow restrain the logic of capital to seek profit, irrespective of racial or national loyalties.

It is important to underscore the fact that the differences of opinion relating to the "Negro Question" are not simply academic. On the one hand, during the 1920s an international conflict between ideas that had greatly transformed world history in a matter of years was being played out in the boroughs of New York and in other U.S. urban centers. Clearly, the mass arrests and deportations of alleged radicals during and after the war—that is, during the first stage of the Cold War led by Attorney General Mitchell Palmer—indicate that the U.S. government understood the stakes were high in a global economy composed of competing economic interests by bourgeois nationalists and Bolsheviks alike. Indeed, World War I, with its mobilization of millions of men and devastating machinery, suggests that "talking politics" in such a period was serious business, not to be engaged in lightly.

On the other hand, Garvey, Du Bois, and the black socialists were earnestly competing with each other over who would lead the black American working class to freedom, variously conceived. The moments of a sense of a "bigger brotherhood" shared between these intellectuals were the exception, not the rule. Aside from the practice of sharply attacking one another in their respective editorial pages, the deep disagreements were manifested in the numerous conventions and organizations jointly and separately convened. Perhaps the most famous case in point is the All-Race Assembly or "Negro Sanhedrin" held in Chicago in 1924. Present at the assembly, whose purpose was to create a program for civil rights in the United States, was an impressive array of black leaders, businessmen, and representatives from the NAACP and the National Urban League, as well as from the ABB and the WP. Significantly, the leadership of the assembly chose not to invite Garvey or his representatives, despite the urgings of the WP. The veneer of unity began to wear thin on the first day of the assembly, when, raising the specter of anticommunism, "the Chicago Mayor William Dever, in his welcoming address, warned the delegates not to listen 'to the colored and white demagogues. Your salvation rests within yourself'" (Hutchinson 18). The black conservative author and Howard University dean who chaired the Assembly, Kelly Miller, also did a fine job shelving the labor issue of utmost importance to the socialists present, until the last day, when the ABB's Otto Huiswood was finally compelled to call out in protest:

> "Dean Miller, you have been sabotaging this convention from the first day. You promised a labor hearing before the convention because it was the most important issue. We demand a hearing. Ninety-five per cent of the members of our Race are workingmen" . . . Miller gaveled and said Huiswood was out of order but members of the audience whose labor sympathies had not been known before began popping up demanding the right of labor to be heard. (qtd. in Allen and Foner 62)

Miller ultimately succumbed to the pressure but then had a committee "revise" the resolutions on labor that the Communists engineered. It is no wonder, then, that both Du Bois (in "The American Scene") and Garvey (in "Negroes Dig Graves for Each Other Under the Guise of Race Leadership") criticized the "Negro Sanhedrin" and that the ABB and the WP organized the American Negro Labor Congress a year later in Chicago precisely to contest the actions of the 1924 assembly. Lovett Fort-Whiteman, a black Communist who was the national organizer of the congress, declared in his keynote address that "[t]he aim of the American Negro Labor Congress is to gather, to mobilize, and to co-ordinate into a fighting machine the most enlightened and militant and class conscious workers of the race in the struggle for the abolition of lynching, jim-crowism, industrial discrimination, political disenfranchisement, segregation, etc., of the race" (qtd. in Allen and Foner 112–13). The battle between black intellectuals intensified and became more polarized as the decade wore on.

The organizational staging of the debates is vital to note because, owing to the thriving black press of the time, African American writers and intellectuals unaffiliated with the organizations could not help but know of the debates. The various political positions informed by nationalism and internationalism circulating at the time in black newspapers and weeklies (such as the *Amsterdam News*, the *Pittsburgh Courier*, the *Chicago Defender*, and the *Baltimore Afro-American*) made available alternative conceptions of identity and cultural work for Harlem Renaissance writers. By rehistoricizing the postwar period in terms of these competing positions, we understand that Renaissance writers did have political choices, albeit choices limited by the options of the period. More specifically, the socialist challenges to the racial and nationalistic ideologies of influential black leaders of the 1920s allow us to reassess the popular perception of the Harlem Renaissance, as well as much black literature, as naturally or logically African and/or American.

2

The Dual Nationalism
of Alain Locke's *The New Negro*

But fundamentally for the present the Negro is radical on race matters, conservative on others, in other words, a "forced radical," a social protestant rather than a genuine radical.

Alain Locke, *The New Negro*

In 1925, Alain Locke published what he hoped would be the founding anthology of the Harlem Renaissance. *The New Negro: An Interpretation* instantly established a literary canon bound by values and interests that, to this day, direct popular views toward African American literature and life. Locke firmly believed the literary works composing *The New Negro* were of great importance, for they embody "a renewed race-spirit that consciously and proudly sets itself apart" (xxvii). Unashamed of their race and culture, his black contributors stand as ideal representatives of the "New Negro," a postwar generation of black Americans whose cultural contributions Locke claimed would strengthen democracy in America. Recent anthologies of Harlem Renaissance literature continue to portray the movement as one devoted to issues of racial expression, black pride, and American social reform. In this regard, *The New Negro* has been a tremendous success; its impact can still be felt.

But the popularity of Locke's conception of the New Negro is largely the effect of ignoring the many other voices intensely engaged in debates over issues of black identity, culture, and politics during the 1920s. More precisely, *The New Negro* should be contextualized in terms of the important

postwar ideological fight between advocates of black nationalism, socialism, and American capitalism who struggled to position themselves as
leaders of working-class black Americans. Through their respective cultural fronts, each faction sought to define the politics of the New Negro.
At stake was whether the black masses—many of whom were radicalized
by the failed promises of World War I, the racist backlash of the Red
Summer, and the political reverberations of the Bolshevik Revolution—
would continue to support American capitalism or, conversely, embrace
black nationalism or socialism as solutions to racism and class inequality
in America.

Locke's introduction to and editing of The New Negro skillfully intervenes
in this debate over the politics of postwar black Americans. He proves to
be a wary navigator between what he must have viewed as the Scylla and
Charybdis of socialism and black nationalism. And yet, Locke appropriates
the rhetoric of the Left and the black nationalists—indeed, at times representing himself as both an advocate of the rank and file and a national
awakener—while he simultaneously excludes from his anthology virtually all of the writings published in radical black journals. Consequently,
The New Negro narrowly comprises literary works that, taken as whole,
confirm Locke's own desire that the New Negro possesses a black national
identity and a patriotic loyalty to American capitalism that transcends class
differences and interests. In other words, The New Negro anthology participates in the dominant anticommunist, nationalistic discourse following
World War I that hoped to banish the specter of communism from the
politics and culture of working-class blacks.

Locke was quite aware that his anthology was an intervention into the
postwar debates about the politics and culture of the new generation
of black Americans; he justly subtitles the book "An Interpretation." He
premises his particular interpretation of the New Negro on his progressive redefinition of the concept of race. Influenced by the anthropological
studies of Franz Boas and his students, such as Melville Herskovits (whom
he anthologizes in The New Negro), Locke argues against genetic or biological determinist notions of race. In an essay he published shortly before
The New Negro, entitled "The Concept of Race as Applied to Social Culture"
(1924), he redefines race as a strictly social category. He views race—or
what he terms "social race"—as historically determined, the result of
"social heredity" (191), or inherited "cultural conditions," "stressed val-

ues" (194), and a "tradition, as preferred traits" (195). As Locke states, "Instead therefore of regarding culture as expressive of race, race by this interpretation is regarded as itself a culture product" (193). Locke's view that race is social helps us to situate The New Negro as a symbolic political act in itself, since the anthology is an attempt to create a "tradition" of "stressed values" and "preferred traits" that will shape the way in which black Americans view themselves.

Significantly, the concept of "social race" squares nicely with the post-war ideologies of nationalism. In fact, Locke's usage of "social race" is a synonym for "nation," since integral to modern nationalist projects is the identification of common circumstances, traditions, cultural traits, and values that constitute nationhood. Locke consciously substitutes the con-cept of race for nation as early as 1916 when, at a lecture at Howard University, he argues that "[w]hat men mean by 'race' when they are proud of race, is not blood race, but that kind of national unity and national type which belongs properly not to the race but to the nation" ("Racial Progress and Race Adjustment" 86). In this sense, Locke tells us that his own "race pride" is a kind of "national" pride, based on the unity he felt with other people of his "national type." As a project that aims to preserve, promote, and defend the black national culture, The New Negro represents Locke's desire to foster national pride among black Americans.

Locke's nationalist view of race is immediately apparent in his fore-word to The New Negro. He conflates the terms race and nation in the key word "self-determination" that he uses to describe the political and cul-tural aspirations of the New Negro (xxv). He explains that he takes his comparison of the "racial awakening" of the New Negro from "those nascent movements of folk-expression and self determination which are playing a creative part in the world today" (xxvii). He goes on to argue that, "[a]s in India, in China, in Egypt, Ireland, Russia, Bohemia, Palestine and Mexico, we are witnessing the resurgence of a people" (xxvii). This comparison implies that black Americans are somehow a separate nation (like India, China, and so forth) within the American nation, suggesting the postwar view that "peoples" are more abundant than empires, which, consequently, makes sense of his other comparison of black Americans as like those "emergent nationalities" (xxv) budding around the world after the breakup of the great, multinational empires. Locke may have been influenced by the nation within a nation thesis found in some of Cyril Briggs's and the African Blood Brotherhood's articles published in the early 1920s. Most likely, his implication is the product of a process of reasoning set going by postwar nationalistic discourses. Locke also uses the figure of "awakening" central to nationalist rhetoric, a figure that implies the black nation-race, like other nations, has been dormant and, upon awaking, will rise to reclaim its immemorial heritage and fulfill its historic destiny. Indeed, as David Levering Lewis notes, "Locke sought to graft abstractions for German, Irish, Italian, Jewish, and Slovakian nationalism to Afro-America" (117).

It is not surprising, then, that Locke would need to identify a capital for his imagined national/race community, since nationalist projects always speak of territory and lay claim to a geographical center for their realization. For Locke, Harlem "is—or promises at least to be—a race capital," which has "the same role to play for the New Negro as Dublin has had for the New Ireland or Prague for the New Czechoslovakia" (7). Harlem provided Locke with a black population density and, more important, a center of cultural expression that could function to ethnicize blacks internationally whose consciousness and identity was not sufficiently racial. Harlem will lead to a greater "race-welding" (7) by its "stressed values" and "tradition" requisite for the formation of a black social race. Locke believed he was witnessing the birth of the black American race, which has "been a race more in name than in fact" (7)—his anthology would be a birth certificate of sorts for the race. Oddly, most of the contributors to *The New Negro*, including Locke, were from places other than Harlem, which thus renders Harlem solely a symbolic place of birth for the cultural nationalist literary movement.

Since Locke attempts to graft abstractions of other nationalisms onto the New Negro, the New Negro movement necessarily bears a striking resemblance to other traits of European nationalism. I have already noted Locke's messianism, to which we can add here that, since black Americans represent an African advanced guard, they have a duty to enlighten African peoples and to rehabilitate "the race in world esteem" (14), as well as to aid Africa in its future development (15). Another defining trait of the nationalistic New Negro is his "folk" character and expression. Locke, along with other contributors such as Montgomery Gregory and Arthur Huff Fauset, imbues his discussions of the New Negro with the notion of the folk, and in "Negro Youth Speaks" Locke seems almost beside himself with the folk spirit he writes about. The young black writers, Locke claims, "dig deep into the racy peasant undersoil of the race life" (51). Beneath their modernistic styles, he perceives "the instinctive gift of the folk spirit" evident in Jean Toomer's "folk-lilt" and "glamorous sensuous ecstasy," Claude McKay's "peasant irony" and "folk clarity," and Rudolph Fisher's "emotional raciness" (51)—concepts for the most part absent although implied in the somewhat less nationalistic *Survey Graphic* version of the book published earlier in the same year. Locke's essay is in the vein of late eighteenth- and early nineteenth-century Romantic nationalism, in spite of his claim that the writers, like "gifted pagans," "return to nature, not by the way of the forced and worn formula of Romanticism, but through the closeness of an imagination that has never broken kinship with nature" (52). How the young writers, who were not peasants by birth, residence, or occupation, have an unbroken "kinship with nature" goes unexplained, and, in fact, cannot be explained except as a fantasy cultivated by an intellectual elite. The most "peasant" of Harlem Renaissance writers was McKay, who was raised on a farm in Jamaica but whose family was literate, landowners, and members of a local elite. As Eric Hobsbawm notes in *Nations and Nationalism Since 1780*:

> since the later eighteenth century (and largely under German intellectual influence) Europe had been swept by the romantic passion for the pure, simple and uncorrupted peasantry, and for this folkloric rediscovery of 'the people,' the vernacular languages it spoke were crucial . . . more often than not the discovery of popular tradition and its transformation into the 'national tradition' of some peasant people forgotten by history, was the work of enthusiasts from the (foreign) ruling class or elite. (103–4)

A student of German Romanticism, Locke revives the Romantic idealization of the "folk" and the poets' supposed relationship with that "folk," in order to establish a historical and natural precedent for his nationalistic conception of the New Negro cultural movement. And like other anti-Enlightenment philosophers of nationalism (Gellner 66–71), he necessarily privileges "vitality," "feeling," and cultural specificity over notions of universality based in rationality. The value of cultural specificity is particularly important here, since Locke, as well as other contributors, expresses interest in recuperating black vernacular traditions as visible signs of the origins of the race-nation. For Locke, "[t]he Spirituals are really the most characteristic product of the race genius as yet in America" ("The Negro Spirituals" 199).

The political meaning of the nationalism of *The New Negro* emerges most clearly in Locke's attempt to distance himself from socialism. One indication that Locke considered the socialists undesirable political contenders is that he fails to mention the existence of the African Blood Brotherhood (ABB), the Communists' Workers Party (WP), or the black Socialists by name or organization. Yet the pressures of the black Left leave a trace on Locke's political characterization of the New Negro, which, like most discourses, must be read dialogically. He characterizes the New Negro as committed to "the ideals of American institutions and democracy" (10), namely to American capitalism. To postpone momentarily the question of whether or not he was right, I suggest that such a statement is intended to be not only sociological but also, as relating to Locke's political goals, prescriptive. We sense the rhetorical force of a seemingly simple statement of fact when he follows it with a discussion of how the new "creed" of "race co-operation" among blacks arose spontaneously as a defense and offense against prejudice (11). He is careful to assure his reader, however, that the reaction to racism "is radical in tone, but not in purpose and only the most stupid forms of opposition, misunderstanding or persecution could make it otherwise" (11). He goes on to dismiss the Left from his anthology of 446 pages (in the first edition) with the following few words: "Of course, *the thinking Negro* has shifted a little toward the left with the world-trend, and there is an increasing group who affiliate with radical and liberal movements. But fundamentally for the present the Negro is radical on race matters, conservative on others, in other words, a 'forced radical,' a social protestant rather than a genuine radical" (11, emphasis added). Note that he begins by discussing "the thinking Negro" and ends with a political assessment of black Americans in general. His earlier discussion about "the few" who "know that . . . the vital inner grip of prejudice has been broken" (4) suggests that the New Negro might actually encompass a rather small minority of the black population. In short, the New Negro anthology represents the New ("thinking") Negro and, logically, should also represent the new left-wing ("thinking") blacks who were, by Locke's own estimation, increasing in number in response to a world trend. Instead, he assures his reader that, as a "forced radical" on racial matters, the New Negro should be differentiated from the "genuine radical"; he is careful not to imply that the New Negro in any way agrees with the socialists' criticism of the capitalist basis of racism and class inequality in America. Locke concludes his point by characterizing left-wing blacks as fabricating "quixotic radicalism" (11), and he excludes the multitude of radical prose, fiction, and poetry he could have culled from Randolph and Owen's *Messenger*, the ABB's *Crusader*, or the CPUSA's *Daily Worker* published since the war. One could argue that the black Left constituted a minority and Locke's goal was to be representative. However, the handful of black writers he champions (particularly Hughes, McKay, and Countee Cullen) were far from being representative, since, as scholars of the Harlem Renaissance have shown, they were part of an elite (in education, class, or affiliation) relative to the black masses (Huggins 305–6).

If we consider some of the ways that other black intellectuals interpreted the New Negro, we better appreciate the conservatism that informed Locke's definition and selection of material for his anthology. As one might expect, the black Socialists' interpretation of the political character of the New Negro greatly differs from that of Locke's. In 1920, A. Philip Randolph and Chandler Owen took up the issue of the New Negro in an editorial they published, entitled "The New Negro—What Is He?" Locke would agree with their assertion that the New Negro stands "for absolute and unequivocal '*social equality*'" (73); yet the gulf widens between the Socialists and Locke when we read that, for the former, the New Negro is primarily a worker who

> would repudiate and discard both of the old parties—Republican and Democrat. His knowledge of political science enables him to see that a political organization must have an economic foundation . . . As workers, Negroes have nothing in common with their employers. The Negro wants high wages; the employer wants to pay low wages. The Negro wants to work short hours; the employer wants to work him long hours. Since this is true, it follows as a logical corollary that the Negro should not support the party of the employing class. (74)

Randolph and Owen also shuttle between description and prescription, yet the conclusions of their argument are dramatically different from

Locke's political assessment of black Americans. Implicit in their definition is the Socialist's critique of American and black nationalism: the
workers' structural position under capitalism and their class identification
fracture national identifications with the ruling class and produce an international, working-class identity. Consequently, Randolph and Owen
maintain that black nationalists are deluded since they believe they can
abolish the systemic problems of capitalism by creating a black bourgeoisie and state loyal to the race. Since Randolph and Owen's New Negroes
comprehend their class positioning and interests, they are much more
politically savvy and left wing than Locke's. Their class consciousness necessarily makes them radical on matters other than race.

Similarly, Cyril Briggs, head of the nationalist-socialist ABB, defines the
New Negro as politically militant and Left (particularly after the riots in
Tulsa and elsewhere) when he writes, "The Old Negro and his futile
methods must go. After fifty years of him and his methods the Race still
suffers from lynching, disfranchisement, jim crowism, segregation and a
hundred other ills. His abject crawling and pleading have availed the
Cause nothing. He has sold his life and his people for vapid promises
tinged with traitor gold . . . The New Negro now takes the helm" ("The
Old Negro Goes" 9). According to Briggs's definition, Locke would be
classified as an "old Negro" who plays it safe by dismissing the militant
radicalism of the New Negro as quixotic, delusionally battling the industrial mills of capitalism as if they were dragons. And while Briggs is conservative in some ways on "race matters"—notably his biological
definition of race—he does not share Locke's conservatism on the question of the New Negro's Americanism. Hence, in an editorial he wrote
for the *Crusader*, entitled "Two Negro Papers Discuss Americanism," Briggs
fumes:

> Much maudlin nonsense has been written about Americanism in the
> Negro press recently, and the thinking Negroes have been forced to sit
> in shame while servile and idiotic editors emulated the great American
> spirit—the great American spirit of the lynching bee, the jim-crow car,
> the ghetto, the partial court of 'justice,' and the many other vile features
> of that spirit. But the Negro press is not all servile. Our editors are not all
> blind idiots—or worse. And at last Americanism is being discovered and
> interpreted in its true light.

He then quotes from the *Pittsburgh American* and Chicago's *Whip*, the latter which reads in part: "Americanism! Is that the vile and bloody thing that paraded in Washington, in Omaha, in Chicago, in Springfield and in Tulsa? Americanism! Is that the hideous creature who masquerades in skull and bones calling himself the Ku Klux? Americanism! . . . Is that the thing which lynches, burns, and murders the weak? If so, then give us Lords and Kings with guillotines and dungeons" (10). In fact, like Randolph and Owen, Briggs argues that capitalism fosters nationalism among the working classes: "Capitalism . . . knows neither prejudice nor nationality, save the brands it seeks to foster for its own benefit among the workers" (qtd. in Taylor 10), an opinion that obviously diverges from Locke's unproblematic presentation of the New Negro's patriotism.

Furthermore, as the quotation from the *Whip* suggests, we need not only cite avowedly left-wing intellectuals to assess better whether or not postwar black Americans were as conservative as Locke makes out for his rejection of socialism. For instance, in an article entitled "The New Negro" published in the *Oklahoma City Black Dispatch*, Roscoe Dunjee takes issue with claims circulating in the press at the time that black Americans who fight back against discrimination and persecution have been influenced by the International Workers of the World (I.W.W.) or the Bolsheviks. For Dunjee, the New Negro's radicalism arises spontaneously and, not simply confined to "race matters," extends into a critique of the racist U.S. legal system as a whole:

> I think you ought to know how the black man talks and feels at times
> when he knows that you are nowhere about, and I want to tell you, if
> you were to creep up to-night to a place where there are about 10,000
> Negroes gathered, you would find no division on this one point, I know
> that they would all say, "WE HAVE NO CONFIDENCE IN WHITE POLICEMEN."
>   Let there be one hundred or one hundred thousand, they would with
> one accord all say, WE HAVE NO CONFIDENCE IN THE WHITE MAN'S COURT.
> (66)

The famed World War I black lieutenant of the 367th U.S. infantry William N. Colson writes in a similar vein about black America's radicalism in an article he published in the *Messenger* entitled "The New Negro Patriotism" (1919). Like Locke, he begins with a seemingly exclusive category of the "thinking Negro" and ends by including most blacks, although, again, with different results: "Intelligent Negroes have all reached the point where their loyalty to the country is conditional. The patriotism of the mass of Negroes may now be called doubtful" (69). The articles by both Dunjee and Colson confirm the leftward shift among black intellectuals but contradict Locke's dismissive comment that the shift is only "radical in tone, but not in purpose" (69). There is no reason to believe that these and other radicalized black intellectuals did not mean what they said about the structural inequalities of postwar America and their lack of patriotism.

One lesson we learn from rehistoricizing Locke's pronouncements on the New Negro vis-à-vis some of the other interpretations of the period is that Locke's progressive rhetoric of nationalism conceals (perhaps insufficiently) his identification with the bourgeoisie. Indeed, one of the greatest challenges the socialists presented to Locke and other bourgeois-identified black leaders was that the black working class (already radicalized by the war and postwar discrimination) would ally with white workers under the banner of socialism and act *by themselves* to limit (through reform) and eventually to destroy (through revolution) the American class system. Hence, Locke, as well as a number of the contributors to *The New Negro*, emphasizes the cultivation of a black elite (sufficiently trained with the principles of free enterprise and bourgeois democracy) who would assure that the black working class continues to be "radical on race matters, conservative on others" (11). Arguments for the need of *multiracial, working-class* unity are conspicuously absent. Instead, multiracial unity should only be cultivated among the elites (or a "Talented Tenth") of the country, for, as Locke warns, "the only safeguard for mass relations in the future must be provided in the carefully maintained contacts of the enlightened minorities of both race groups" (9). In other words, as Huggins aptly puts it, "[t]here was nothing wrong with American society that interracial elitism could not cure" (115).

The names and employment of many of the contributors Locke chose for his anthology speak volumes: Charles S. Johnson (editor of the Urban League's *Opportunity*), James Weldon Johnson (executive secretary of the NAACP), Kelly Miller (dean of the College of Arts and Sciences at Howard University), Robert Russa Moton (president of Tuskegee and the Negro Business League), Walter White (assistant executive secretary of the NAACP), Elise McDougald (Urban League, U.S. Department of Labor),

W. E. B. Du Bois (NAACP), Eric Walrond (business manager of *Opportunity*), and so forth. Moreover, their academic credentials are stunning, representing a host of private and Ivy League schools, which include Harvard, Brown University, Howard University, Cornell University, University of Chicago, Columbia University, and Fisk University. Trained by and affiliated with an intellectual elite, the contributors understandably were suspicious of those who promoted working-class leadership and self-determination, including the formally uneducated and "unrefined" Garvey.

A number of essays in part 2 of *The New Negro* suggest that black Americans should be directed into predominantly black institutions of higher education (namely Howard and Hampton-Tuskegee) and black commercial and cultural communities (such as Durham and Harlem) to safeguard the proper formation of their cultural nationalist and assimilationist identities. As Robert R. Moton writes in his contribution to the anthology, "the strongest recommendation that Hampton and Tuskegee have is the character and service of the men and women whom they have trained for the leadership of their people" (332). Or, as Kelly Miller writes of Howard University, "[i]ts essential objective from the beginning has been to develop a leadership for the reclamation and uplift of the Negro race through the influence of the higher culture" (313). (In part 1, Montgomery Gregory also argues for the need of a "national Negro Theatre" for playwright, musician, actor, dancer, and artist [159]). Even Du Bois, in his powerful contribution on the relationship between colonial domination and the racist exploitation of "domestic" labor, does not argue for the need for a multiracial working-class movement, a position consistent with his well-intended but nonetheless paternalistic view of liberation. Du Bois, who gets the final word in the anthology, assures the reader that the growing movement of Pan-Africanism against imperialism and colonial domination has its "main seat" of leadership in the United States (411)—in other words, in the leadership of the NAACP.

Yet Locke's adherence to bourgeois nationalism stops short of black nationalism proper; he straddles the fence between socialism and Garveyism. His adoption of the principles of postwar nationalism, particularly the notion of self-determination for the race-nation, is more rhetorical than substantive. Locke's grafting of the model of Dublin onto Harlem is meant to invoke, not provoke, a political movement among blacks for self-determination. Thus, his reference to "Harlem's quixotic radicalism" includes Garveyism, which he rejects for essentially the same reason he rejects socialism, that is, it does not comprehend the allegiance blacks have or should have to America as an idealized democratic nation: "American nerves in sections unstrung with race hysteria are often fed the opiate that the trend of Negro advance is wholly separatist, and that the effect of its operation will be to encyst the Negro as a benign foreign body in the body politic. This cannot be—even if it were desirable. The racialism of the Negro [like his radicalism] is no limitation or reservation with respect to American life" (12). Just as he omits socialist literature, so he excludes overtly black nationalist literature from *The New Negro*. After all, plenty of writers were producing it at the time, particularly in the pages of Garvey's *Negro World*. As Tony Martin tells us, "[t]he writing of poetry was little short of an obsession with Garveyites . . . Poetry was a regular feature of the *Negro World*" (43). Hence, the prolific black nationalist poets of the *Negro World*, such as Ethel Trew Dunlap, Leonard I. Brathwaite, and J. Ralph Casimir, whose poetry equals if not surpasses in form much of the poetry that Locke champions, find no place in the national community of *The New Negro*. Garvey's "Back to Africa" program simply contests Locke's bourgeois-assimilationist desires.

Conceivably, Locke could have omitted any allusion to the socialists and Garveyites, thereby further insulating his interpretation against his ideological opponents. Yet Locke's subtle allusions to socialists and Garveyites serve rhetorically to frame his desired interpretation of *The New Negro*: they function as threats to the white elite concerning their fortunes and the future of America. Thus, when he writes of the American "wants" and "ideas" of black Americans, he warns that "we cannot be undone without America's undoing" (12), suggesting that U.S. political and economic rulers must legally recognize the rights of blacks to be offered what American capitalism has to offer, or else they may face some form of revolution ("undoing"). We also find a threat in his warning that "Harlem's quixotic radicalisms call for their ounce of democracy to-day lest to-morrow they be beyond cure" (11). Locke offers his cultural nationalist-assimilationist program or else anarchy (spread by the "incurable disease" of radicalism). More precisely, we can say that strategically he raises the specters of Garveyism and socialism to frighten the bourgeoisie into making the main concessions he wants, which, to follow Charles S. Scruggs's argument, include a privileged place for him as one of the black political elite. Locke's postwar historical moment provided him with a prime opportunity to make such an argument, which, in another period (such as ours) would not have any of the rhetorical force.

Moreover, Locke's adoption of the nationalist rhetoric so vital to the Garveyites can be understood as an attempt to co-opt the political sympathies of the movement, particularly among the younger generation of whom he was very fond, and to redirect the black nationalist impulses along safer paths. The texts of those contributors who had been directly influenced by Garvey (such as Zora Neale Hurston, Walrond, and J. A. Rogers) and indirectly influenced (such as Hughes in his back-to-Africa-sounding poem "Our Land," for example), are reinterpreted by Locke to suit his particular position in the debate. Like many petit-bourgeois nationalists, he creates a myth of a mighty movement of support behind him, composed of both southern peasants and urban intellectuals, to make his own pronouncements all the more authoritative and convincing.

As Jeffrey C. Stewart points out in his introduction to a collection of Locke's lectures given at Howard University in 1916, "Compared with the political nationalism advanced by Marcus Garvey in the early 1920s, Locke's New Negro arts movement must have seemed a relief to educated whites" (xlvi–xlvii). And, as I have argued, Locke's particular matrix of nationalism must have seemed much safer than the political programs of the WP, the ABB, and the black Socialists, notwithstanding the fact that the latter had moved to the political center by 1925 and, in truth, no longer presented an ideological threat to American capitalism. Locke was careful to exclude literary works of the two political movements that challenged his cultural nationalism and Americanism. Relative to Garveyism and socialism, the contributors all seem to suggest that blacks in the United States should identify themselves as "American," albeit of a "different shade" (Herskovits 353).

This model of an essentially unified black intellectual community in the pages of The New Negro does not come, however, without its share of internal debate. In fact, there are two extremes from Locke's position represented in "Negro Art and America" by Albert C. Barnes, the white millionaire collector of African art, and "The Negro's Americanism" by Melville Herskovits, the Boasian anthropologist. Simply put, Barnes represents blacks as "old Negroes" and Herskovits represents them as "no Negroes." Barnes regurgitates a host a racial stereotypes: black Americans are "a primitive race" possessing a "primitive nature"; they are "poet[s] by birth" (19); and, forever filled with joy and song, they live poetry "in the field, the shop, the factory" (20)—a fine lesson for those exploited white workers who complain about their prosaic lives! Herskovits rejects any notion that black Americans are innately or even culturally a different race from other Americans. Writing about his visit to Harlem, he notes that what he "was seeing was a community just like any other American community. The same pattern, only a different shade!" (353).

Perhaps it is puzzling why Locke would include essays that blatantly contradict his notion of "social race." But the racial characteristics Barnes praises and the Americanism upon which Herskovits gloats are two sides of the same coin, tendered for the purposes of advancing Locke's goal of making the cultural movement safe for those from whom he asks recognition. In other words, the differences of argument between the contributors are circumscribed by their adherence to a dual nationalism, best characterized by the current term of "African American." The apparent diversity of perspectives reaches a consensus that "blacks" and "Americans" have together and/or separately the following criteria to constitute a race/nation: common ancestries, common experiences, common psychologies, and common cultures, all of which are conceived as equal to or better than other races/nations. Put differently, all agree that blacks in the United States constitute a separate race and/or are members (even if provisionally excluded) of the separate American nation.

We witness the dual nationalism at work throughout the anthology. Other examples of the contributors' racial classification of black American identity and culture include William Stanley Braithwaite's identification of an "artistic temperament and psychology precious for itself" of black Americans (29); J. A. Rogers's claims about the "atavistically African" sources of jazz and ragtime (217); and James Weldon Johnson's assertions that the "unique characteristics" of "movement, color, gayety, singing, dancing, boisterous laughter and loud talk" are "typically Negro" (309). The fiction and poetry support and supplement these observations, so that in the selections by Hurston, Toomer, and Fisher we find race portraits that (among other things) define blacks as essentially different from white Americans. Or in the poetry of Cullen, Hughes, and Toomer we find references to an African soul ("The Negro Speaks of Rivers" 141), an

African "dark blood" that courses through the New Negro's veins ("Heritage" 205), and African "[r]ace memories" ("Georgia Dusk" 136), respectively. While these elements are not necessarily nationalistic (as in the case of Hurston, for instance), they function together (particularly because of Locke's framing) as criteria of nationalist identification; they are protonational elements, which in the hands of Locke, are transformed into a cultural nationalist appeal. Adapting Etienne Balibar's analysis of the characteristics of nationalism to black literature, we find narratives that posit the existence of an "invariant substance" (86)—soul or blood—and that represent the New Negro as the culmination of a long historical process of coming to consciousness of a special destiny. In nationalist fashion, black writers project their "individual existence into the weft of a collective narrative, on the recognition of a common name and on traditions lived as the trace of an immemorial past (even when they have been fabricated and inculcated in the recent past)" (Balibar 93). The very desire to create racial slice-of-life stories corresponds to the nationalist representational desires of the so-called new nationalities proliferating after the war.

Aside from Herskovits, the other contributors who emphasize the "Americanness" of blacks include Paul U. Kellogg, James Weldon Johnson, and Hughes. In "The Negro Pioneers," Kellogg, the editor of the *Survey Graphic*, characterizes the Great Migration to the North as "an induction into the heritage of the national tradition, a baptism of the American spirit that slavery cheated him out of" (277). Similarly, Johnson writes that "Harlem talks American, reads American, thinks American" (309). But perhaps Hughes says it best when he writes, "I, too, am America" ("I Too" 145). Thus, virtually every contribution works to define blacks on this nationalistic/racial axis. Nationalism is the ideological limit beyond which Locke and his New Negro compatriots, as represented in the anthology, do not pass.

Locke could have chosen different works by a number of the same contributors, resulting in less of a nationalist and anticommunist consensus. Indeed, as Arnold Rampersad notes, the disputes that a number of contributors had with Locke (particularly McKay), illustrate that "the unity suggested by *The New Negro* was mainly a front presented to the world" (xxii). Locke's editorial practices thus function to reaffiliate politically a number of the writers, making inconsequential some of their socialist and black nationalist affiliations. Aside from Eric Walrond, who frequently contributed to Garvey's *Negro World*, W. A. Domingo contributed to Randolph and Owen's *Messenger*, Langston Hughes to the Communists' *Workers Monthly* and the *Messenger*, and Claude McKay to virtually every radical magazine of the period. Domingo's socialist articles present a picture of him far different from the one Locke frames for his readers. Critical of notions of racial or national loyalty, Domingo writes in the *Messenger*: "The owners of jobs have common interests and pay only as much wages as they are forced to pay. Their interests are opposed to those of their employees. And color or race makes no difference. Jews underpay Jews, and Negro employers rob their employees regardless of race or color. The interests of all workers are alike" ("A New Negro" 145). Similarly, a number of the poems Hughes published in socialist magazines, such as "Johannesburg Mines" and "Steel Mills," address, however inadequately, issues of class and exploitation under capitalism. In retrospect, given his aspirations, Locke was right to keep the debate in the pages of *The New Negro* within bourgeois-nationalist boundaries, since Charlotte Osgood Mason, one of his wealthy white patrons, did not tolerate any truck with radicalism, as evident in her withdrawal of patronage from Hughes when he openly expressed his Communist sympathies by publishing "Advertisement for the Waldorf-Astoria" in 1931.

From this perspective, *The New Negro* is symbolically a black convention—a kind of textual "Negro Sanhedrin." Locke does as good of a job controlling the debate over definitions of black Americans and the political options to overcome racism as had his anticommunist and antilabor friend and colleague from Howard University, Kelly Miller, chairman of the "Negro Sanhedrin" or All-Race Assembly of 1924. Even though the purpose of the assembly was to create a program for civil rights in the United States, Miller forestalled discussion of the labor issues important to the socialists in attendance, and then had a committee revise (that is, distort) the Communists' resolutions on labor. Perhaps Locke's well-publicized opposition to propagandistic poetry, expressed in articles such as "Our Little Renaissance" (1927) and "Art or Propaganda" (1928), should be read in light of his own particular political agenda. Unlike those socialist and black nationalist writings not represented in *The New Negro*, the literature Locke includes does not make topical references to the politically explosive issues of the postwar period. Instead, we find labor and racial issues dealt with generally or fictionally at a distance. For example, none of the poetry he includes is as sharply critical of the well-publicized murder of several black workers in Jasper County, Georgia—killed by their employer for supposedly corroborating with a Federal investigation into their debt-peonage—as is Dunlap's "The Peonage Horror" (1921), published in the *Negro World*. Jasper County, Dunlap bluntly writes, is "[w]here the slave trade thrives as in the days of yore" (qtd. in Martin 53). Locke's most emblematic omission of labor issues is his replacement of Mahonri Young's striking drawing of "The Laborer" from the New Negro number of the *Survey Graphic* with a Winold Reiss portrait of Charles S. Johnson—suited, bespectacled, impeccably bourgeois. The heightened nationalist and therefore conservative tenor of *The New Negro*, relative to the *Survey Graphic* version, indicates Locke's desire to legitimize the cultural movement for a middle-class readership who he assumed would rather see an unthreatening intellectual than a towering, muscular worker—equipped with what appears to be a potentially dangerous hoe.

Even when Locke allows entrance to a socialist poet like McKay, he carefully censors him so as not to offend the ruling classes, particularly those residents of the White House who had an impressive record in the 1920s for simultaneously enacting racist legislation and crushing labor unions and the Left. Locke's revision of the title of McKay's poem "The White House" to "White Houses" greatly changes the meaning of the poem, a militant protest against the U.S. government's discriminatory laws. (William Stanley Braithwaite's essay seems to second Locke's move to silence radical poetry when he states his preference for the aestheticism of McKay's "The Harlem Dancer" over the propagandism of "If We Must Die" [40]). It is Miller's essay in *The New Negro* that sounds the keynote of the anthology: "Howard University must keep the race spirit courageous and firm, and direct it in harmony with ideals of God, country and truth" (322).

Undoubtedly, the contributors to *The New Negro* were profoundly committed to overcoming racism in America by supporting and developing a black culture that could challenge the racial stereotypes of the time. At question in this chapter are not the good intentions of the contributors but rather the ways they define the New Negro and, by implication, their means and goals of creating a truly egalitarian society free of racism. As I have argued, the selected works that constitute *The New Negro*, carefully framed by Locke's introductory essays, collectively elide many vital questions raised by the black socialists, such as whether blacks can be defined primarily according to one of the postwar nationalisms, or whether they should identify themselves within any nationalistic framework whatsoever. Locke's editorial role in the making of The New Negro effectively turns a lively dialogue about the identity and political options of black Americans into a monological paean to a relatively conservative New Negro. The New Negro, in short, ends up being "radical in tone but not in purpose."

3

The Dance of Nationalism in the Harlem Renaissance

The American Negro must remake his past in order to make his future.

Arthur Schomburg, "The Negro Digs Up His Past"

A people may become great through many means, but there is only one measure by which greatness is recognized and acknowledged. The final measure of the greatness of all people is the amount and standard of the literature and art they have produced. No people that has produced great literature and art has ever been looked upon by the world as distinctly inferior.

James Weldon Johnson, The Book of American Negro Poetry

While Alain Locke was perhaps the most important dual nationalist ideologue of the Harlem Renaissance, he certainly was not the only one. He could never have achieved his editorial coup had he lacked the support of other black writers who also shared his perspective of the New Negro. Indeed, many writers of the period subscribed to Locke's belief in the power of a national literature to effect a progressive ideological change in America. Certainly, such idealism must have been highly attractive to a generation of writers (most born around 1902) who sought to make an impact on American society and letters.

To be sure, many writers of the Harlem Renaissance used their literary talents to create personas, characters, themes, and plotlines that represented cultural nationalism and/or Americanism as the primary means by which African Americans should define themselves and pursue their goals of freedom. In numerous Renaissance texts, racial destiny structures narrative development, atavism reveals true character, sadness stems from national "exile" from an unknown but desired African homeland, and happiness is found by embracing one's racial/national duality as an African and an American. We also discover the overriding political dialogic between socialism and nationalism present in much of this literature as well. Yet, here too socialism is subsumed and in a contradictory relationship to the more powerful nationalist ideology of the 1920s, resulting in some texts with an emergent class consciousness nonetheless contained by the categories of race and nation. As a way of demonstrating some of the linkages between the politics and the literature of the period, this chapter will analyze select texts by four major writers of the movement, namely Countee Cullen, Langston Hughes, Jesse Fauset, and Claude McKay. It is my contention that the writings of these authors articulate both the political aspirations and determinations that make the Harlem Renaissance an important, although historically limited, modern African American literary movement. They reveal how nationalism distorts and at times subverts the very critiques of racism, sexism, and class inequality Renaissance writers otherwise advocated in their work.

Countee Cullen may not be the first writer who comes to mind when one thinks of the most race-conscious and proud writers of the Harlem Renaissance. Indeed, Cullen took unpopular positions among those writers who asserted the existence and value of a uniquely racial literature. Fully aware of his minority position, Cullen boldly states his preference for English poetic conventions in a foreword he wrote to his anthology of poetry by black Americans entitled *Caroling Dusk* (1927): "As heretical as it may sound, there is the probability that Negro poets, dependent as they are on the English language, may have more to gain from the rich background of English and American poetry than from any nebulous atavistic yearnings toward an African inheritance" (xi). In a review he wrote of Hughes's first major book of poetry, *The Weary Blues* (1926), Cullen goes so far as to suggest that "jazz poetry" is an oxymoron ("Poet on Poet" 73). Henceforth, he viewed the emerging careers of vernacular poets like Hughes as doubtful. "If I am going to be a poet at all," Cullen proclaimed, "I am going to be a POET and not a NEGRO POET. This is what has hindered the development of artists among us" (qtd. in Early 23). Ultimately, Cullen's defense and use of traditional poetic forms (such as the sonnet, the Spenserian stanza, and the ballad) were linked to his defense of himself as a poet, a difficult profession for black Americans, since many critics still believed that blacks could not be poets, let alone first-rate poets. He anticipates the surprise that the literary establishment may express on encountering *Color* by beginning the book with the lyric "Yet Do I Marvel," wherein he marvels that God would "make a poet black, and bid him sing!" (3).

Nevertheless, Cullen could not and did not escape the cultural nationalist atmosphere of his day. He too had his contradictions and also contributed his share of racial and cultural nationalist prose and poetry to the movement. In his foreword to *Caroling Dusk* (1927), Cullen also expresses a sentiment similar to that of James Weldon Johnson when he writes: "The place of poetry in the cultural development of a race or people has always been one of importance; indeed, poets are prone, with many good reasons for their conceit, to hold their art the most important" (x). In these lines, too, we find the slippage of meaning between "race" and "people" and, hence, by implication, between "race" and "nation." Granted, as Gerald Early rightly notes, Cullen did not have a black nationalist agenda since he did not assert that African Americans have a separate culture or language (40), one of the criteria of Wilsonian nationalism. Nonetheless, Cullen's poetry expresses a concept of "a race or people" that underpins ethnic cultural nationalist projects. In particular, he distills the thematic of the rediscovery of an essentially heroic black self, history, and destiny. Perhaps his strongest poem on this topic, second only to the often-anthologized "Heritage" (1925), is "The Shroud of Color" (1924), later republished in his first book of poetry, *Color* (1925).

"The Shroud of Color" begins by establishing the Du Boisian formulation of the problem of the twentieth century as it is subjectively experienced by an individual black man: deeply injured by the injustices of the color line, the black protagonist wants to die. Cullen's transformation of Du Bois's "veil" of color into a "shroud" suggests his protagonist's profound sense of hopelessness. Cullen's nameless protagonist in "The Shroud" is a social product of a racist culture that brands the lives of blacks as inferior and worthless. Desperately praying to God in a moment of severe existential crisis, the suicidal protagonist laments: "Lord, being dark, forewilled to that despair / My color shrouds me in, I am as dirt / Beneath my brother's heel" (26). This man has so internalized his oppression that he experiences his despair as "forewilled." Cullen makes clear that his protagonist's suffering mostly stems from his alienation from and humiliation by others (or "brothers," to cite Cullen's use of the filial trope).

Like T. S. Eliot's aimless modern man in The Waste Land (1922), Cullen's protagonist has not learned how to "sacrifice" himself to a cause greater than his own individualistic struggle for happiness (Cullen 26). He believes he lacks bravery "to pay the price / In full" for his happiness, let alone to pay the price of saving his own life. Above all, the protagonist feels doomed because he lacks a sense of black history and a tradition of political struggle to which he can sacrifice himself. He has not yet discovered the Garveyite bigger brotherhood. The poem proposes that only a racial historical sense (certainly a far cry from Eliot's Greco-Roman and Anglocentric tradition) will enable him to reconceptualize his individual struggles in relation to the implied blood brotherhood and provide him with a reason to live. Thus, in Shelleyian fashion, imagistically reminiscent of The Triumph of Life (1822), Cullen has God grant the protagonist a series of visions leading to his comprehension of his black identity, history, and destiny.

But the protagonist's salvation is hard won, since his first two visions leave him relatively unmoved from the grave's edge. He first witnesses the universal struggle to survive found in nature: "all was struggle, gasping breath, and fight. / A blind worm here dug tunnels to the light, / And there a seed, racked with heroic pain, / Thrust eager tentacles to sun and rain" (29). These visions transmogrify into a Hobbesean "state of nature," ruled by "the ancient fundamental law / Of tooth and talon, fist and nail and claw" (30). Even though he extracts the lesson that "no thing died that did not give / A testimony that it longed to live" (31), he remains enshrouded by his color since the vision of human struggle is solely composed of the same race of "white" people that torments him and have power to struggle.

After these secular visions of survival fail, Cullen's God turns up the heat, so to speak, by showing the black protagonist a vision of God and his "great warriors" casting out Lucifer from heaven (32); yet the man is unmoved by this display of good over evil as well. While he feels privileged to witness this celestial event, the protagonist suggests that the lesson is lost on him, since as a mortal he cannot identify with Christ, and surely not with such a militant fighter against a force seemingly more formidable than racism. Still suffering from his socialized sense of racial inferiority, he cries, "Why mock me thus? Am I a god?" (33). In other words, he cannot locate himself on the Great Chain of Being, since he does not identify with either beasts, white people, or angels. The failure of these visions suggest but do not yet clearly articulate his forthcoming revelation that the shedding of the shroud of color—the symbol of the "forewilled" death of the black man in a racist America—will not involve losing one's racial identification. On the contrary, the process of coming back from the grave involves a nationalist awakening to one's true racial identity.

Consequently, only his final vision of black people discloses to him a reason for living. Cullen composes the first part of this vision with idyllic images and primitivist stereotypes of an ancient Africa:

> Now suddenly a strange wild music smote
> A chord long impotent in me; a note
> Of jungles, primitive and subtle, throbbed
> Against my echoing breast, and tom-toms sobbed
> In every pulse-beat of my frame. The din
> A hollow log bound with a python's skin
> Can make wrought every nerve to ecstasy,
> And I was wind and sky again, and sea,
> And all sweet things that flourish, being free. (33)

Like the persona of "Heritage," the protagonist finally recognizes his essential African identity when he contemplates his ancestry, although here, unlike in "Heritage," the contemplation abolishes his sense of racial and national alienation. Significantly, his spiritual homecoming is triggered by hearing the "wild music" of Africa, for it helps us to situate Cullen in relation to other Harlem Renaissance writers who also imparted to African culture and especially music the power to revive the atavistic racial memories "long impotent" within oneself. In addition, the "sobbing" of tom-toms suggests the Garveyite articulation of black sadness as the result of denying one's true identity while living in "exile" in the white-dominated wasteland. And equally noteworthy is that the "return" of his racial self is equated with a "re-transformation" of his self into nature. Cullen's description of his protagonist's "homecoming," in short, is rife with Romantic-nationalist tropes, bordering on racist discourse, that associate African Americans with nature, vitality, and a "primitive" freedom from the restraints of Western civilization. He replicates these primitivist tropes in other poems such as "Pagan Prayer," "Fruit of the Flower," and "Atlantic City Waiter," the latter which depicts a black waiter whose movements betray "[t]en thousand years on jungle clues" (10).

Once his revitalizing vision of African return abruptly ends, the protagonist witnesses scenes of slavery—"the cry the lash extorts, the broken breath / Of liberty enchained" (33)—that teach him he does not suffer alone. It is here, amid the slaves' "harmony of faith in man" (33), that he discovers he has "courage more than angels have" (34), suggesting that the previous parallels between heroic angels and black men (or conversely Lucifer and racism) were not without some truth. That is, his identification with oppressed yet rebellious black people precipitates a new sense of self worth and suggests that he also has a divine purpose in life. More generally, Cullen's poetry suggests that the black ego, weakened by racism, repairs itself by learning about black heroes. In "Black Majesty" (1929), Cullen illustrates this when he begins the poem with the lines, "These were kings, albeit they were black, / Christophe and Dessalines and L'Ouverture; / Their majesty has made me turn my back / Upon a plaint I once shaped to endure" (200). Since the ego ideal is formed through identification with the parents, and especially the father for the male child (as Freud argues in *The Ego and the Id*), the protagonist's identification with his black "forefathers" is central to his psychological salvation. The racialized identification represents his ascension to "manhood" and initiation into an African bigger brotherhood.

This crucial formative process of racial identification is followed by the true nationalist moment of the poem, the liquidation of the individual subject into the racialized "people": "The cries of all dark people near or far / Were billowed over me, a mighty surge / Of suffering in which my puny grief must merge / And lose itself; I had no further claim to urge / For death" (34). His newly acquired perception of his Pan-African identity and history places his "puny grief" into the larger narrative of Africa's struggle for freedom. Cullen equates nationalist consciousness with religious consciousness: mortality is overcome—or at least the issue of dying is suspended—as one merges with the deathless national community.

(Also noteworthy in this context is that the suspension of time is a pre-condition for the protagonist's entire vision [29], suggesting the homogeneity of time central to nationalist ideology [Anderson 28–3 1].) Cullen also metaphorizes his awakening as an African homecoming (34), a spiritual, if not a material, return to Africa. Most important, it is the mystical nationalist view of collective identity and destiny that saves the protagonist from suicide. No longer "forewilled" to despair, his life has become inscribed within a seemingly divine nationalist narrative. Cullen's counteracting of the narrative of racism with nationalist narrative transforms the individual black subject, made insignificant by racist discourse, into the messianic subject of history. He comes to embody the liberating telos characteristic of bourgeois-democratic nationalist discourse. In a word, having sloughed off "the shroud of color," he discovers he is the "universal Negro."

While Cullen may have arguably produced one of the best cultural nationalist poems of the Harlem Renaissance, Langston Hughes's work from the 1920s participates more fully in the dominant ideology of the times. Aside from his well-known poem of African spiritual return entitled "A Negro Speaks of Rivers," the last section of Hughes's first volume of poetry, The Weary Blues (1926), is particularly instructive for an understanding of his Renaissance nationalism. "Our Land" includes previously unpublished poems evocative of Garveyism. The opening poem, which shares the section title, expresses desire for, once again, an idealized African homeland:

> We should have a land of sun,
> Of gorgeous sun,
> And a land of fragrant water
> Where the twilight
> Is a soft bandanna handkerchief
> Of rose and gold,
> And not this land where life is cold.
> We should have a land of trees,
> Of tall thick trees
> Bowed down with chattering parrots
> Brilliant as the day,
> And not this land where birds are gray. (99)

As in the work of Du Bois and Garvey, we find the longing for the African *Gemeinshaft* reassert itself—a desire for an organic community where subject and object, folk self and nature are reunited. By desiring a reunification with nature, the Romantic-nationalist Hughes also suggests that African Americans have what Locke referred to as a "never broken kinship with nature" ("Negro Youth Speaks" 52). The association of black Americans with nature and nature with Africa runs throughout Hughes's Renaissance poetry, including such poems as "The Negro Speaks of Rivers," "Dream Variation," and "Poem," the latter which reads: "The night is beautiful, / So the faces of my people. / The stars are beautiful, / So the eyes of my people. / Beautiful, also, is the sun. / Beautiful, also, are the souls of my people" (58). The black folk, so conceived within this ideological framework, are undifferentiated by class or ideology, but, instead, are awash in Hughes's compensatory aestheticization.

However, unlike the Garveyites, Hughes expresses pessimism regarding a return home to his heart's desire. Consequently, "Our Land," which also genders as feminine the desired African motherland of "love and wine and song," turns into a lover's lament. In the last stanza, the persona cries, "Oh, sweet, away! / Ah, my beloved one, away!" (99), signifying his estrangement from the African motherland. In the end, he wants to banish the thought of Africa as a way of banishing the ache of nationalist desire. Thus, for Hughes, "our land" also represents a Garvey-like exile from and longing for the motherland but without the possibility of actual return.

The repressed returns, however, and in Hughes's poetry it especially returns in the nightlife of urban black clubs. Hughes posits the Harlem nightclub—the place where music, dance, and drink supposedly weakens the restraints of "white civilization"—as a center of expression for African American culture, even more so than the black church. If one reads *The Weary Blues* from back to front, the structure of Hughes's thinking becomes clear: the first section of the volume of verse, bearing the same name as the book, presents black New York club life as emblematic of a uniquely African American culture. It is here at night and in clubs (symbolic for the black unconscious and the reemergence of "instinct," seen through the lens of a racial psychology) that race memories and desires are given freer play. So, in "To Midnight Nan at Leroy's," Hughes's view of a girl named Nan dancing to a blues song in a "*Jungle night*" with a "*Jungle lover*"

(30) is suggestive of the return of the African repressed within the white world (*their* land) "where birds are gray" ("Our Land" 99). The concluding section of "Our Land," in contrast, formulates the problem (that is, being trapped in "white civilization" and longing for Africa) that in turn explains the origin and meaning of the African American cultural forms found in "The Weary Blues" section and scattered throughout the entire volume. As a way of rejecting the racist devaluation of blacks in American culture, Hughes thus couples his aestheticization of African Americans with the construction of black national spaces characterized by African-inspired activities that provide meaning to life.

The return of the repressed African self is premised on the belief in the existence of a putatively innate (if at times unconscious) African self. Like Cullen, Hughes bases his belief in an essential African identity on the popular pseudoscientific theories of biological determinism that equate blood with identity or character. "All the tom-toms of the jungle beat in my blood," Hughes writes in "Poem," "All the wild hot moons of the jungles shine in my soul" (102). By relying on the tropes of primitivism popular with other writers of his generation (Cooley), "Poem," for example, develops the motif that "civilization" is a facade that hides a primitive self and world. "I am afraid of this civilization—," Hughes reveals, "So hard, / So strong, / So cold" (102). In "Lament for Dark Peoples," Hughes goes so far as to metaphorize civilization as a "circus cage" into which blacks are "herded" and on display for the white world's entertainment (100).

However, one should underscore that, departing from Garvey, Hughes did not embrace separatism. He ends the "Our Land" section and thus *The Weary Blues* with his "Epilogue," later anthologized as "I, Too." "I, Too" is his Whitmanian-Du Boisian affirmation of his American identity—"our land" is also America. Thematically, Hughes thus compensates for the loss of an African homeland with the discovery of an African-American one, remaining squarely, like many of his contemporaries, between modern twentieth-century nationalisms.

Hughes's Renaissance poetry is nationalistic in another important respect: he eagerly heeds James Weldon Johnson's call for black nationalist poets who could create a uniquely black aesthetic. Drawing an analogy between the budding Harlem Renaissance and the Irish Renaissance, Johnson urges, "What the colored poet in the United States needs to do is something like what Synge did for the Irish; *he needs to find a form that will express the racial spirit by symbols from within*" (*The Book of American Negro Poetry* 41). By wanting to find a national language expressive of "the racial spirit," Hughes conveys the Romantic nationalist valorization of the folk's vernacular. As Hughes succinctly states in his influential essay "The Negro Artist and the Racial Mountain" (1926), he wants to write poetry "racial in theme and treatment" (308). He argues that white American culture (figured as the "racial mountain") is an impasse to developing a black aesthetic. In particular, he finds middle-class black artists, who have been educated to emulate white culture, in denial of their racial identity and heritage. (His implied targeting of Cullen is not completely fair, as "The Shroud" suggests.) In contrast to the assimilated black middle class, working-class blacks are the repositories of an authentic black culture, since they "still hold their own individuality" and can furnish black artists with the proper subject (black life) and expressive forms (jazz, blues, spirituals, and folk music) (306). Hughes unmistakably sounds here like William Wordsworth in his preface to his second edition of *Lyrical Ballads* (1802) and even reiterates the binary opposition between the soul-numbing city and the invigorating vernacular culture and expressive forms of the folk. Hughes concludes that the chief responsibility of the black writer is to produce a racial literature drawn from African American life and culture. "We younger Negro artists who create," Hughes defiantly writes, "now intend to express our individual dark-skinned selves without fear or shame" (309).

Hughes's concern with depicting the lives of working-class and lumpen proletarian black Americans in a "superstructural" form of their own (Gates, *Figures in Black* 30) suggests that he tapped into the postwar nationalist ideology more fully than Cullen and many other black writers. His privileging of black vernacular culture and language, two central criteria for the establishment of ethnic peoplehood, is Wilsonian through and through. Moreover, as a consideration of his virtually blues-less radical poetry from the 1930s suggests, Hughes used the blues form in the 1920s to depict "weary" people politically incapacitated by social oppression and lacking the political consciousness necessary for social transformation. As he writes in a prefatory note to *Fine Clothes to the Jew* (1927), "The mood of the *Blues* is almost always despondency," even though when they are "sung people laugh." Resistance to and freedom from oppression appears only in African American cultural forms, such as black music or religion, and on occasion in poems about suicide and death, such as "Exits," "Prayer for a Winter Night," "Suicide's Note," "Judgment Day," and "Suicide." Indeed, at times Hughes seems to insist on a kind of carpe diem for the black oppressed in the cultural spaces of the black nightclub. "Shake your brown feet, Liza," inveighs Hughes, "(the banjo's sobbing low) / The sun's going down this very night— / Might never rise no mo'" ("Song for a Banjo Dance" 29). In short, Hughes's use of the blues implies his pessimism toward substantial political change in America.

It is also important to note that, as with most forms of nationalism, Hughes's also functions through a hierarchy of race. He represents "Nordic" culture as amorphously homogenous ("Negro Artist" 306), "dull" (307), and implicitly incapable of providing the black artist with anything useful—a notion he dispenses with in the 1930s. Nevertheless, Hughes's chauvinism was simply a small-scale inversion of the colossal ideological system of Eurocentrism that was responsible for initiating and justifying some of the greatest crimes against humanity. What Frantz Fanon states about the colonized peoples' attempts to create a national culture very much applies to the efforts of Hughes and many black American writers in the 1920s:

> The Negro, never so much a Negro since he has been dominated by the whites, when he decides to prove that he has a culture and to behave like a cultured person, comes to realize that history points out a well-defined path to him: he must demonstrate that a Negro culture exists. And it is only too true that those who are most responsible for this racialization of thought . . . are and remain those Europeans who have never ceased to set up white culture to the fill the gap left by the absence of other cultures. (212)

In other words, Hughes's own racialization of thought lead him to believe that a superior black art must come from a superior black race; he could not answer, however, how one can possibly promote social equality with unegalitarian ideas.

In spite of being ideologically boxed in by the dominant nationalist discourses of the time, Hughes was not deaf to the socialists' calls for a class-conscious literature. Hughes had read and published a few poems in the socialist magazines of the period. In fact, he had always written what we could call a proletarian political poetry, that is, a poetry that deals directly with working-class problems and issues of social justices. Yet, in the 1920s, he was unable to transform his criticisms of social injustice into a poetry that goes beyond the reification of oppression, whether by "God," "fate," "nature," "civilization," or technology. In poems Hughes published in the Communists' *Workers Monthly* and the Socialists' *Messenger*, for example, he abstractly figures the oppressor as a God who serves the rich ("God to Hungry Child"), "Rich Ones" who are "[b]ut foam on the sea" ("Rising Waters" 48), "Death"—"the vilest of whores" ("Poem to a Dead Soldier" 48), and the mills that "grind out new steel / And grind away the lives / Of men" ("Steel Mills" 43). Aside from representing African American workers as the political objects of history, these poems lack the details about class and racist oppression that make his depression-era poetry so powerful. Even the relatively familiar Marxist perspective on exploitation that we find in his "Share-Croppers" poem from the 1930s—that is, that "[w]hen the cotton's picked / And the work is done / Boss man takes the money / And we get none" (185)—is absent from his 1920s poetry. His Renaissance poetry also lacks the political understanding of the solutions to oppression that he was to attain during the "Red Decade." "Saturday Night" (1926), the only pre-Depression-era poem Hughes writes that acknowledges the possible benefit of a communist future ("red dawn"), represents black workers as grooving in a jazz club "till de red dawn come" (88). That is, he once again represents the black folk as politically passive, although culturally active.

In truth, during his Renaissance period, Hughes could not resolve the problem he represents in the poem "Johannesburg Mines" (1925): how to write a poem about the *class* oppression of black workers? Or as he writes in "A Song to a Negro Wash-woman" (1925), which movingly depicts the life of a black woman caught in racist domestic servitude, "I have many songs to sing to you / Could I but find the words" (41). Undoubtedly, Hughes searched for a means of expression, but, importantly, he was writing without much of a challenge to his cultural nationalist perspective. After all, during his most productive phase in the middle of 1920s, the *Messenger* had already veered right of center, the *Crusader* was defunct, and the Communist Party was not yet in a position to organize and nurture writers. As I have been arguing, the nationalist and cultural nationalist leaders were in the stronger position to define (black) identity

and culture for young writers such as Hughes and Cullen. Hughes remained stuck fast in the contradiction he apparently perceived between a
nationalist view of oppression and a class analysis of oppression. To bor-
row from Raymond Williams's useful discussion of what he terms "the
complex interrelations between movements and tendencies both within
and beyond a specific and effective dominance" (*Marxism and Literature*
121), Hughes's left-wing sensibilities were at best *emergent* but not *dominant*, owing to the cultural and political contexts in which he wrote.

Whereas Hughes's youthful work struggles to articulate nationalist
modes of resistance to racism, the early writings of Jesse Fauset focus on
the ways in which nationalism can serve the interests of black women
who are doubly oppressed by being black and female in a patriarchal and
racist society. As the literary editor of the *Crisis* between 1919 and 1926,
Fauset resided at the hub of black nationalist discourse of the decade.
Fauset's interest in questions of nationalism is at first evident in the jour-
nalistic articles she wrote for the *Crisis* during the early 1920s. She accom-
panied Du Bois to Europe as one of the black American delegates of the
Second Pan-African Congress in 1919. While there she was exposed to a
wide range of political leaders from London, Brussels, Paris, and Geneva,
the various locales that hosted the Congress. With a Wilsonian conviction,
the "Manifesto of the Second Pan-African Congress" forthrightly proclaims "[t]he absolute equality of races—physical, political and social"
(5) and the need for African self-determination. Du Bois strategically
staged the congress contemporaneously with the Paris Peace Conference
as a way to pressure the victorious powers to grant the rights of national
self-government to Africans. On her return to the United States, Fauset
wrote an article for the readers of the *Crisis* on her impressions of the
congress. In this piece, she expresses her enthusiasm for the work accom-
plished, as well as her sense of her own Pan-African identity. "We were
all one family in London," she writes. "What small divergences of opinion, slight suspicions, doubtful glances there may have been at first were
all quickly dissipated. We felt our common blood with almost unbeliev-
able unanimity" ("Impressions" 12). Later she relates that after the delegates from several parts of Africa, Grenada, Martinique, Jamaica, India,
and the United States had accepted Du Bois's resolutions, those present
"clasped hands with [their] newly found brethren and departed, feeling
that it was good to be alive and most wonderful to be colored. Not one

of us but envisioned in his heart the dawn of a day of new and perfect African brotherhood" (13). Rhetorically, little differentiates these words of Fauset from those of other black nationalists of the 1920s, such as Du Bois, Marcus Garvey, or Cyril Briggs, in spite of some of the important political differences between them. In fact, her refunctioning of the filial trope—the rhetoric of family—is central to black nationalist discourse in its attempt to provide a biological basis (that is, "blood") for the nation, empire, or blood brotherhood. And she ends the piece with a sentiment one also finds in the polemics of militant black nationalists some forty years later: "All the possibilities of all black men are needed to weld together the black men of the world against the day when black and white meet to do battle" (17–18). She strikes a similarly militant chord in her article "Nationalism and Egypt," where she writes expectantly that Egypt's struggle for independence from British Imperialism is representative for "the whole dark world" (316).

The impact of the great events taking place around the world and among black communities in the United States finds its way into her first novel, There Is Confusion, published in 1924. There Is Confusion is typical of literature of the Harlem Renaissance in the sense that characters consciously explore their African American heritages and found their identities upon heroic black figures of the past. From the start of the novel, Joanna Marshall, the female protagonist, looks for primarily black role models with whom to identify, such as Frederick Douglass, Denmark Vesey, Harriet Tubman, Phillis Wheatley, and Sojourner Truth. Like Countee Cullen and Langston Hughes, Fauset illustrates just how necessary such role models are for surviving and excelling in an atmosphere of racist contempt. In one scene Joanna speaks to Peter Bye, her significant other: "'Colored people,' Joanna quoted from her extensive reading, 'can do everything that anybody else can do. They've already done it . . . They've been kings and queens and poets and teachers and doctors and everything. I'm going to be the one colored person who sings the best in these days, and never, never, never mean to let color interfere with anything I really want to do'" (45). The novel's proof of Joanna's assertions is one we also encounter in the writings of Du Bois, Garvey, and others: in spite of appearances, history is intrinsically fair, since it has an egalitarian telos. Or, as Joanna's father consoles her: "All people, all countries, have their ups and downs . . . and just now it's our turn to be down, but it will soon roll around for our time to be up" (19–20). Note again the typical semantic slippage between the concept of "people" and "country" that is characteristic of nationalist discourse of the Harlem Renaissance. Once again we see that "it is the magic of nationalism to turn chance into destiny" (Anderson 19).

Throughout most of the novel Joanna "marshals" her strength and ambition to be a great dancer and singer. Significantly, the chosen career of this middle-class woman is sustained by her "natural" childhood attraction to "[a]ny sort of folk-song or dance" (18). Fauset reproduces the nationalist privileging of the folk culture and identification that putatively cuts through class divisions and class identifications. Thus, when she and her sister Sylvia see the black children on Sixty-third Street singing and dancing to the folk song "Barn! Barn!," Joanna is transported outside of her own class identity and urban social conditions and back to some essential racial self. She insists on participating, and the children, "with the instinct of childhood for a kindred spirit" (48), let her join in. She is so moved by the song and dance (structured by call and response) that after returning home she shares it with her family and friends. The meaning of her "transport" (47) becomes clearer when we read that Peter's performance of the melody on the piano had "a haunting, atavistic measure" (49), suggesting that Joanna's "kindred spirit" originates from ancient Africa, and, by implication, from an agrarian or peasant economy. And Joanna's chance discovery of the folk song and her racial self does not end here. With a destiny only nationalist histories and fiction can provide, her dream later in the novel "to do a dance representing all the nations" (100) comes true when she gets the part of the "colored American" in a production called "The Dance of the Nations." And, not surprisingly, her choice of song to represent black America is none other than "Barn! Barn!" Hence, in step with Romantic nationalist ideology, the highly refined, middle-class, and urbanized Joanna discovers her true black folk self.

Yet, very much in the camp of the assimilationist NAACP during the 1920s, Fauset tempers her black cultural nationalism with Americanism. A number of times we read how the black characters put country before race, in order, finally, to uplift the race. Against her future brother-in-law's plea that she should "build up colored art," Joanna cries in astonishment: "Why, I am . . . You don't think I want to forsake—us. Not at all.

But I want to show us to the world. I am colored, of course, but American first" (76). She gets a chance to represent herself as an all-American (232) when the white dancer quits her role as the "white" and "red" American. For the white American role she must wear a white mask, which simultaneously affirms and denies her cultural difference—her double identity as black and American. When prompted by an audience member to take it off, she does. In response to the initial astonishment of the audience, she proclaims: "there is no one in the audience more American than I am" (232), echoing Du Bois's recurrent claim on Americanness. The sign of her Americanism is that of heroic sacrifice to the greater good of the nation: her great-grandfather, she explains, fought in the Revolution, her uncle in the Civil War, and her brother fights in Europe.

The theme of sacrifice to the race and/or nation is central to the logic of the novel, climaxing at its end. As Joanna says, "You've got to renounce something—always" (284). Vera Manning, who "passes" most of the novel, in the end sacrifices the pleasures of her racial incognito to live in the South as a black woman to "serve," "help," and "heal" her "own folks" (270). Maggie sacrifices herself to serve in France with the YMCA to aid black soldiers at the front (258). After the war she dedicates her life to nurse the dying Philip (266), who "died for his country" when, as we are told, he really wanted to live for his country (288).

The supreme sacrifice in *There Is Confusion* is Joanna's, and it is here that we find the novel's nationalism most subtly at work in two of the often unspoken tenets of nationalism: religious mysticism and sexism. Joanna's quick acceptance of Peter's request to give up her career (284), her simultaneous realization of "her true [domestic] self" (291), and her belief that Peter is the "*fons et origo* of authority" (292), all suggest that Fauset's ideal black woman finds her highest calling as mother and wife. Indeed, she depicts Joanna as blissful in her marriage, yet this sacrifice of hers is not without ambition: "She was still ambitious, only the field of her ambition lay without herself. It was Peter now whom she wished to see succeed" (292). Her goal is to make a "man" of Peter (283) and, by extension, a man of her son (284–85), so that they may carry on the work of making the black race great and the American nation better. In other words, she offers herself—her own feminist aspiration—as a sacrifice to family, race, and nation. Fauset's sentiment doubles that of the *Negro World* female contributor who announces that the role of the black mother and wife is to support the black man's desire to build a black nation (Parham 8). Thus, contrary to what some critics have seen as a contradictory ending to the novel, by giving up her career Joanna enters more fully into the "great tradition" of black heroes that she aspires to from the beginning: like them, she realizes that her own individual ambitions are not as important as living and dying for one's "people," "race," or "nation." It is the future as represented by her son that she lives for, which thus makes her life continuous with the past and future. What Anderson says about the religious dimension of nationalism in a secularized world applies to Joanna as well: "What . . . was required was a secular transformation of fatality into continuity, contingency into meaning" (19). And, historically, as Etienne Balibar argues, the family (alongside the schools) is the primary institution within which nationalist identities and values are transmitted generationally, thus making motherhood heroic and ideologically central to the nationalist project (100–103). Critically, her concerns for women's rights are undercut by the patriarchal basis and the religious mysticism of the nationalist vision. Thus, her nationalist rhetoric of self-sacrifice to race and nation proves to be the Achilles heel of her feminism. In this sense, Fauset is representative of the historical contradictions of nationalism as a discourse of human rights in the Harlem Renaissance.

The influence of nationalism, as well as its antiliberatory contradictions, is also evident in the poetry and political writings of Claude McKay. Even though McKay was a socialist during the heyday of the Harlem Renaissance, he is one of the most consciously nationalist writers of the movement, bearing the weaknesses of the quasi-nationalist Leninist line on subject peoples that comes to dominate the Communists' understanding of the "Negro Question" in the 1930s. McKay's writings from the Harlem Renaissance are testimonials to the virtual inescapability of nationalist thinking for politically conscious writers of the postwar period.

As has been well documented, a few years after arriving in the United States from his native Jamaica, McKay fell in with the Socialists and the *Liberator* crowd, such as Max Eastman, Mike Gold, Joseph Freeman, John Reed, Floyd Dell, and William Gropper, and began publishing his poetry in the magazine. In 1921 he accepted an invitation to join the *Liberator* staff as both a correspondent and a coeditor (Tillery 48). A few years later McKay decided to break with the Socialists and the magazine because he claimed that they were unwilling to confront the "Negro Question" as a question separate from that of class. McKay, it appears, had been swept up by discussions of the "National and Colonial Question" going on in the Communist movement and among the African Blood Brotherhood.

We see an early influence of the quasi-nationalist Leninist line on his thinking in an essay he wrote for the *Workers' Dreadnought*, the London Communist weekly, entitled "Socialism and the Negro" (1920). Here he affirms that "the Negro question is primarily an economic problem" (51), but he defends his qualified support for the nationalism of Garvey on these grounds: "Although an internationalist Socialist, I am supporting the movement, for I believe that, for subject peoples, at least, Nationalism is the open door to Communism" (54). Comparing the Garveyite movement with the nationalist movements in Ireland and India, he adds: "In these pregnant times no people who are strong enough to throw off an imperial yoke will tamely submit to a system of local capitalism." In other words, he expresses a developmental view of revolution that maintains that nationalist anti-imperialist struggles necessarily lead to an anticapitalist politics, an idea painfully refuted during the period of anticolonialism some twenty-five years later as well as up to the present.

In an essay he wrote a year later for the *Liberator*, "How Black Sees Green and Red" (1921), he begins by commenting on how he participated in a Sinn Fein demonstration in Trafalgar Square and was "filled with the spirit of Irish nationalism!" (58). While McKay later attests to his Communist principles, he remains under the sway of the nationalist "folk spirit." McKay argues that he identifies with the Irish because he is also a subject person and, since he "was born and reared a peasant," "the peasant's passion for the soil possesses me, and it is one of the strongest passions in the Irish revolution" (59). His vision of communism, it turns out, resembles that of Romantic nationalism. Or, put differently, McKay suggests that nationalism and communism exist on the same continuum, and at the heart of both is recognition of the inalienable right of self-determination for "peoples," defined by their "passion for the soil" of their respective homelands. "For my part," reveals McKay, "I love to think of communism liberating millions of city folk to go back to the land" (61), the beloved nationalist *Gemeinschaft*.

McKay expresses Romantic nationalist sentiments in much of the poetry he wrote during the 1920s. On the one hand, as an émigré in the

United States and a former Jamaican nationalist, he longs for Jamaica. He demonstrates his strong identification with Jamaican peasants and folk culture in his two collections of dialect poetry, Songs of Jamaica and Constab Ballads, both published in 1912. On the other hand, in his Harlem Renaissance poetry he diffuses his love of his homeland into a generalized longing for Africa. He plays out this theme in "The Tropics of New York" (1920), "Flame-Heart" (1920), "In Bondage" (1920), "Enslaved" (1921), and "Adolescence" (1922), among other poems. In these poems he yearns for an unnamed place, but a place defined by its rural landscapes, or, at a minimum, by an absence of a modern urban environment. His love of nature and disdain for "civilization" is expressive of his black nationalist identification, since he identifies civilization with "[t]he white man's world of wonders" ("Enslaved" 121). Thus, like Cullen and Hughes, as well as others such as Jean Toomer, Gwendolyn Bennett, and Gloria Douglas Johnson, he creates a rather rigid and mystifying binary between nature or Africa and the city or America.

The various nationalist elements of his thought are compounded in "Outcast" (1922). The first two quatrains of the poem read:

> For the dim regions whence my fathers came
> My spirit, bondaged by the body, longs.
> Words felt, but never heard, my lips would frame;
> My soul would sing forgotten jungle songs.
> I would go back to darkness and to peace,
> But the great western world holds me in fee,
> And I may never hope for full release
> While to its alien gods I bend my knee. (121)

These lines are suggestive of atavism; like Cullen's "Heritage" published a few years later, the black persona suggests that he has a visceral (not cognitive) ancestral memory, if one may speak of such a thing. The poem blends religious and nationalist discourses in the figure of the transcendental or ahistorical African soul that longs for its origins, typecast in terms of patriarchy. Yet, like other writers of the ultimately integrationist Harlem Renaissance, McKay suggests that he cannot return to Africa, since he is held "in fee," perhaps because he, as Cullen puts it, "belong[s] to Jesus Christ, / Preacher of humility" ("Heritage" 252). In any case, to invoke Hughes, the speaker feels "caged" by civilization or "the great western world" and exiled from the homeland he never knew.

The remaining quatrain generates an even greater sense of irreparable despair, stemming from the problems of racial alienation and national exile: "Something in me is lost, forever lost, / Some vital thing has gone out of my heart, / And I must walk the way of life a ghost / Among the sons of the earth, a thing apart" (121). It is not only that he has been separated from Africa, but also, worse, knowledge of Africa has been taken from him. This then explains why the regions from which his "fathers came" are "dim" and why he has no cognitive memory of Africa. He is like a "ghost," not fully African, "a thing apart." And it is noteworthy that he casts himself as "a thing apart" from "the sons of the earth," thus underscoring that he is like a son without a known father or mother, an orphan of sorts, forcibly taken from his parents and estranged from his brotherhood by the white imperialist states. Hence, the concluding couplet—"For I was born, far from my native clime, / Under the white man's menace, out of time" (121). Clearly, McKay expresses an essential black identity undifferentiated by class or circumstance, as well as black nationalist longings that make him feel alienated from his present moment, "out of time." His identification of the source of the problem as the "white man's menace" rings of the Garveyites rather than the Communists, who, in spite of their own nationalism, differentiated between working-class and ruling-class "whites," the latter being the "menace" to all workers.

This is not to say, however, that McKay was not at the same time very progressive in his writings on the Russian Revolution and the international working class. In fact, the small book he wrote on American blacks while visiting the Soviet Union for the Fourth Congress of the Third Communist International in 1922, *The Negroes in America*, represents an important contribution to resolving the "Negro Question" from a Marxist perspective. As he writes, "one must organize the Negroes and draw them into the sphere of class struggle" (5). The main vehicle for the politicization of black workers is nothing other than the Communist Third International (5–6). He also expresses criticism of bourgeois nationalism as a possible solution (6) and "the large, apathetic mass of 'one-hundred-percent American' workers who must [also] be turned towards international class struggle" (90).

And, of course, McKay published internationalist poems, most notably "Birds of Prey" (1920), as well as powerful indictments of racist institutions and practices, such as "The Lynching" (1920) and "The White House" (1922). To be sure, "Birds of Prey" holds up to this day as one of the most powerful anti-imperialist poems of the modern period. The birds of prey are nothing other than the imperialist air forces that use violence to protect capital investments: "Squawking in joy of feeling safe on high, / Beating their heavy wings of owlish gray. / They scare the singing birds of earth away / As, greed-impelled, they circle threateningly, / Watching the toilers with malignant eye" (23). McKay expresses his internationalism by telling how the imperialists attack workers who "may be black or yellow, brown or white" (23), that is, regardless of race, when it serves their "greed-impelled" interests. The poem strongly suggests that the multiracial proletariat do have common interests as well as a class enemy in common whom they could do well to live without.

I would argue that a further consideration of his internationalist writings only underscores the power that nationalism (and its attendant ideologies, such as primitivism) had even on the most progressive black and white writers. Moreover, the political contradictions expressed in McKay's work were only symptoms of a larger historical contradiction that plagued the Marxist-Leninist Left in the 1920s, and, as we will see in the subsequent chapters, in the 1930s as well: how to theorize racial/national identifications while maintaining the goals of internationalism. Like Hughes, McKay could not write himself out of this dilemma with any consistency.

Even such a cursory examination of works written before 1926—the crest of the Harlem Renaissance—reveals the influence of nationalism on black writers. These works illustrate just how interchangeable concepts of race and nation were in the postwar period. Nothing seemed more natural than for black writers to conceive of themselves as belonging to a people, unified by the possession of a common racial history and consciousness. For many Renaissance writers, the bridge back to one's geographically and historically distant homeland is nothing other than the black American folk culture that transmits the racial essence that binds one to one's ancestors. Additionally, a number of these writers express, as a matter of course, that they were as American as can be.

After 1926, this ideological consensus among black writers is more difficult to ascertain, since the political situation had substantially changed, depriving them of some of the nationalist leadership and context conducive to their earlier work. Undoubtedly, Garvey's conviction for mail fraud, imprisonment in a federal penitentiary in 1925, and deportation from the United States in 1927 made his program less credible for writers. Writers began privately and publicly to take sides against each other and the black leadership—a good instance being the publication of *Fire!* by a growing anti-Lockean faction of young black writers. Besides, the war was nearly a decade past, and the Great Depression of 1929 propelled many writers politically left. It is understandable, then, why Fauset's *Plum Bun* (1928) is topically removed from the war, the political movements, and the propaganda they engendered; similarly, Cullen's *Copper Sun* (1927) focuses more on interpersonal relationships. And even Hughes's *Fine Clothes to the Jew* (1927) does not pack the kind of nationalist punch as does *The Weary Blues*. The only possible exception is McKay's *Home to Harlem* (1928), which revels in primitivist depictions of the black working class antagonized by Western civilization.

However, it is also important to note that some Harlem Renaissance works are not as visibly caught up in nationalist thinking. Consequently, and contrary to current common sense, anywhere we find a modern ethnic or racial literature, even if it does not profess its pride, we encounter the imprint of nationalism. To revise Schomburg, Harlem Renaissance writers, who worked hard to produce a literature representative of a "people," nationalistically *remade* their past and present in order to make their future—the moment in which we now look back and find what we may mistake as "our" own imaginary racial and national selves mirrored in and therefore legitimated by the literary movement. The historicity and ideological basis of the Harlem Renaissance, as well as of our own perception of race literature, will become even clearer as we explore the writings of black Communists from the 1930s who viewed nationalism as a problem to be overcome rather than as an ideology to be embraced in the struggle to end racism.

Internationalism and African American Writing in the 1930s

4

Marxism and Black Proletarian Literary Theory

Let us sound the bugle-call for militancy. Let us have strong vital criticism, Marxian criticism. Let us have the poetry of the masses. Let us have an international poetry.

William Patterson, "Awake Negro Poets!"

The postwar optimism and hope for national and racial self-determination began to sour for many black intellectuals by the 1930s. Aside from the failure of Garveyism to deliver on its promises, several nationalist movements became outright fascist and racist and were responsible for the subjugation and murder of millions of people. The examples of the German "National Socialists" and the Italian Fascists (the latter which had been fascist as early as 1922) readily come to mind, but it is also important to note that nationalistic, militaristic, and reactionary governments took power throughout Latin America and in Japan as well. By 1938, only approximately seventeen constitutional and elected governments existed worldwide, down from about thirty-five in 1920 (Hobsbawm, *The Age of Extremes* 112). The United States also had its own fascist movements and demagogues who promoted ethnic nationalist ideology, such as the American Liberty League, the Khaki Shirts, the Silver Shirts of America, the Crusaders for Economic Liberty, Father Coughlin, Huey Long, and, of course, the Ku Klux Klan.

Understandably, black writers, hungry for alternative conceptions of politics and cultural work, and indeed for survival, looked for answers from the political organization that took the most uncompromising stand against racism and economic exploitation in the United States, namely the Communist Party of the United States of America (CPUSA). Of the U.S. political parties of the period, none challenged as effectively the rapid growth of right-wing politics worldwide and, consequently, had as great of an impact on black American writers as had the CPUSA. While the CPUSA's line on nationalism was contradictory—at times fostering its own brand of "revolutionary" nationalism and Americanism—it nonetheless provided writers with important alternative conceptions of black culture, politics, and identity with which to work. Moreover, coupled with the contradictions, the applications of the Communists' theories of nationalism were more situationalist than often recognized, thus leaving writers with more flexibility than imagined in anti-Communist studies of proletarian literature. This chapter will critically outline the permutations of the CPUSA's stance on the national question and the "Negro Question" as well as its impact on the black proletarian literary theorists who helped to define the African American literature of the period. I will argue that, during the first half of the decade, the CPUSA and literary proletarians made valuable theoretical advances concerning nationalism that, as we will see in the remaining chapters, provided Langston Hughes and Richard Wright with rich resources from which to fashion their own insightful critiques of black nationalism.

The origins of the Communists' position on nationalism in the 1930s must be traced to the writings of Joseph Stalin. This may appear odd or even problematic to some, especially since U.S. anti-Communism has made it very difficult for scholars on the political Right and the Left to imagine anything of value in the writings of Stalin. Not surprisingly, Stalin is usually skipped over in discussions of Marxism and the national question. Nonetheless, Stalin's *Marxism and the National Question* (1913), written at the behest of Vladimir Lenin, presents the definition of and essentially the position on nationalism that would guide Lenin's and subsequently the Communist International's (Comintern's) understanding of nationalism for decades. Stalin's theoretical breakthrough culminated in his rejection of the racial criterion of nationhood central to nineteenth- and early twentieth-century nationalist discourse. He defines the nation as "a historically evolved, stable community of language, territory, economic life, and psychological make-up manifested in a community of culture" (12). He historicizes and politicizes nations (9), arguing that they are originally promoted by the bourgeoisie for their class interests (21). Stalin maintains that nations have beginnings and endings and that the days of nations are numbered due to the internationalization of capitalism and history's movement toward socialism (38). While he argues that it is important for socialists to defend the "right" to national self-determination, he also warns against the danger of national autonomy, which promotes divisions between the international proletariat (39). Generally speaking, for Stalin, "When the workers are organized according to nationality they are isolated within their national shells, fenced off from each other by organizational partitions. The stress is laid not on what is common to the workers but on what distinguishes them from each other" (22). The "fencing off" of workers by nationality also leads to class collaboration with the bourgeoisie, the latter who claims to speak of national interests between classes (22). In short, Stalin believed that nations come into existence under capitalism and their autonomy needs to be temporarily respected but that, ultimately, the goal of history and socialism is the abolition of nations and nationalisms.

Lenin, who often eclipses the figure of Stalin in studies of Marxism and nationalism, adopts Stalin's historical analysis in large part. Lenin's theoretical contribution is to argue that the overarching issue for an understanding of the national question is the need to defeat imperialism, the "highest stage of development of capitalism." Under imperialism, Lenin argues, the world is divided into oppressor nations (with large amounts of finance capital and armed forces at their disposal) and oppressed nations (who are the exploited subjects of finance capital and state violence). For Lenin, "the right of nations to self-determination" is an anti-imperialist slogan that all socialists should promote, since not to demand national self-determination is tantamount to supporting the imperialist subjugation of nations.

Lenin claims that, strategically, the demand for national self-determination is also one of many democratic demands that socialists can use to broaden the struggle of the proletariat against the bourgeoisie ("The Socialist Revolution" 4, 6). In other words, Lenin perceived nationalism as a necessary transitional, anti-imperialist stage in the political development of the proletariat on the road to internationalism. Ultimately, vis-à-vis nationalism, the "aim of socialism is not only to abolish the present division of mankind into smaller states and all national isolation; not only to bring nations closer to each other, but also to merge them" (6). This merging could only be achieved by forging through political struggle a broad, internationalist working-class consciousness and movement. While critical of bourgeois nationalism, Lenin maintains that oppressed nationalities should have the right to self-determination and that national federation with a Soviet or imperialist state should be voluntary, not forced. Forced incorporation by imperialist states only results in the growth of nationalism, so by allowing for secession or federation, the Bolsheviks hoped they would promote federation with a politically friendly and supportive Soviet State (Conner 34). And, as Lenin argues, federation itself is "a transitional form to the complete unity of the working people of the various nations" ("Preliminary Draft" 23).

Since the struggles of the proletariat varied from nation to nation, on the basis of whether or not one inhabited an oppressor or oppressed nation, Lenin advocated different political strategies for national communist parties. On the one hand, he argues that in politically and economically advanced capitalist countries (such as those of Western Europe and America), the Communists and the proletariat need to struggle on behalf of the subject nations its own imperialists oppress, including those subject nations within its own country ("The Socialist Revolution" 11–12). The great political failing of the leadership of numerous Western and Central European socialist parties of the Communist Second International (1889–1914) during World War I was their defense of their respective "fatherlands" and hence imperialism. As R. Palme Dutt informs us in *The Internationale*, "[t]he British Labour Party, the French Socialist Party, the German Social-Democratic Party, the Austrian Social Democratic Party, the Belgian Labour Party and the Australian and South African Labour Parties supported the war and their Governments" (132). (Interestingly, the Socialist Party of the United States was one of the few parties that opposed the war.) On the other hand, in semicolonial and colonial countries (such as China, Persia, Turkey) proletarian political struggle should center on supporting "the more revolutionary elements in the bourgeois-democratic movements for national liberation" (Lenin, "The Socialist Revolution" 13). Under the leadership of the Comintern, the colonized working classes' historical and political positioning should make them defenders of nationalism (irrespective of its class basis) and, ideally, friendly to the Soviets ("Preliminary Draft" 23). We thus see that, for Lenin, nationalism was neither intrinsically good nor bad and needed to be evaluated historically and strategically.

At the Sixth World Congress of the Comintern in 1928, an international body of Communists, including a number of black American Communists, elaborated the Stalinist-Leninist position on nationalism into a program that largely determined the CPUSA's handling of the national and "Negro Question" over the next seven years. The Sixth World Congress was particularly instrumental in galvanizing the CPUSA, as well as other parties in the Third International, into a revolutionary communist party whose primary goal was to end the dictatorship of the bourgeoisie and to create a socialist society governed by the working class. It therefore "called for a sharpening of working class struggle on every front," as William Z. Foster recalls in his *History of the Communist Party of the United States;* "The central slogan of the congress was 'Class Against Class'" (266). The Communists believed that since class struggle is inherent to class society, it was better to try to resolve the struggle in favor of the working class rather than to ignore it, the latter option being equivalent to supporting the continued rule of the bourgeoisie.

With regard to the national question, *The Program of the Communist International,* which codified the results of the Congress, drew from Lenin's critique of the dangers of the "nation against nation" ideology of World War I. However, the *Program* also followed Lenin on the value of anti-imperialist nationalism. Hence, it outlines a plan for the support of nationalist movements against the imperialist oppressor states. It asserts that the full political, economic, and cultural development of subject peoples could only proceed with national independence. Thus, under subheading "F" in the section on the goals of a dictatorship of the proletariat, we read that task "a" is the recognition of national self-determination and task "c" is to fight for the "[c]omplete equality of all nations and races" (44). The doctrine of the self-determination of nations necessitated that the Communists support all nationalist movements of oppressed nations, regardless of the class composition of the movements. In this sense, the political circumstances of oppressed nations counted far more than the long-range goals of nationalist movements, in spite of the Communists' urging of newly independent nations to become federated with a union of soviets. It appears that the "Class Against Class" slogan was mainly interpreted in this context as pertaining to any "class" of people against the imperialist class. Thus, they interpreted nationalist struggles of oppressed nations as instances of class conflict with the imperialist ruling classes.

The effects of the Sixth World Congress on the "Negro Question" is readily apparent from the many pamphlets, magazine articles, and books that the CPUSA published during the 1930s on African Americans. Breaking with the tendency among American socialists, including that of Chandler Owen and A. Philip Randolph, to view black workers solely in terms of their class positioning within the capitalist mode of production, the Communists viewed the "Negro Question" as a national question. They believed that black Americans were an oppressed "nation within a nation" in the South and a "national minority" in the North. To their credit, the Communists rejected the pseudoscientific conceptions of race that informed both American racism and black nationalism in the 1920s. "Race," the black Communist Harry Haywood argues, "is merely a factor in the oppression of the Negroes. The difference in color of skin and texture of hair between the two races is utilized by bourgeois theoreticians to found false racial theories for the purpose of justifying and facilitating the oppression of the Negroes" ("The Theoretical Defenders" 38). Instead, the class basis of the exploitation of the black nation by imperialism was paramount, and thus, "[t]he struggle of the Negroes for liberation is a phase of the class struggle of the American working class against imperialism, or in other words, as a class struggle which assumes a national form" (Haywood 39). Veteran Communist M. J. Olgin forthrightly states: "Humanity is not split into races but into oppressors and oppressed. The interests of the Negro nation are inseparably tied up with the interests of the white workers and farmers who suffer under the same masters" (72). Here again we see the semantic slippage between the concepts of class and nation when the concepts are viewed in relation to an oppressor class. In effect, the CPUSA replaced the concept of an oppressed black race with that of an oppressed black nation structurally positioned as an oppressed "class."

Accordingly, whereas Du Bois and Garvey racialized the "Negro Question" and drew up a list of race allies, the CPUSA "classed" and "internationalized" the "Negro Question" and aligned black workers with workers of all shades and oppressed nations everywhere in their attempts to be free from imperialist exploitation. At core, the CPUSA adopted the Russian Communists' model of the national question: American Communists should oppose the Tsarist-like American imperialists who oppress the "peasant" black nation living within its borders. Consequently, the CPUSA argued that African Americans had a right to national self-determination in the southern region where they were most concentrated, namely in the Black Belt stretching from Virginia to Arkansas (originally so-called because of its dark, rich soil). The political savvy of the Communists' formulation lies in the double gesture that is at once internationalist and nationalist: they hoped to counter the appeal of Wilsonian nationalism with an anti-imperialist nationalism while maintaining their long-term socialist goals.

Perhaps contrary to appearances, the Black Nation Thesis was not separatist in theory, since it advocated neither the migration of blacks out of a predominantly "white" northern America nor the expulsion of whites from the southern Black Belt. Rather, the issue was that of power relations, that is, of expropriating white landlords and establishing a black, peasant dictatorship. Moreover, the CPUSA defenders of the Black Nation Thesis made it clear that black and white working-class unity before and after a proletarian revolution was of central importance, and that it was hoped that the "Negro Republic" would freely federate with a Soviet America (Ford and Allen 32).

In retrospect, however, the Communists befuddled their program by confusing racial and class politics. It appears that color/culture counted more than class in this model, or rather, they viewed the hypothetical black republic as intrinsically oppositional to American imperialism, and it thus acquired the status of a revolutionary political organization. The CPUSA's willingness to downplay the issue of political economy—that is, whether one should even fight for the establishment of a potentially black bourgeois republic in the South—skirts the issue of working-class self-determination. Under a black bourgeois republic, as Randolph and Owen argued in the 1920s, the black working class would still be beholden to capitalists who, by definition, profit by extracting surplus value from their wage-laborers; periodic economic crises would make even the "loyalist" or most patriotic bosses heartless in laying off workers. In other words, the Communists mistakenly promoted the belief that the black working class could self-determine its existence even within a black bourgeois republic. While they understood that class struggle often does assume a national form under capitalism, they reinforced nationalism within the black working class instead of sufficiently critiquing the limitations of the nation form. Moreover, such a position bred the kind of white distrust of working-class blacks that the CPUSA otherwise worked hard to mitigate, since, even though it rejected the divisiveness of race theories, it reinforced the divisiveness that comes from elevating cultural difference to national difference deserving of state power. Nonetheless, in spite of their limitations, as documented in Robin D. G. Kelley's *Hammer and Hoe* and the autobiographies of black Communists such as Harry Haywood and Hosea Hudson, the CPUSA's center staging of the issues of race and racism in the United States spurred it to launch massive antiracist reform campaigns for African Americans and, in the process, won over many black workers, writers, and intellectuals to the Party. The highly publicized legal defense of the "Scottsboro boys" (nine black youths unjustly accused, tried, and imprisoned in Alabama for allegedly raping two white women) by the CPUSA's International Labor Defense was one result of their antiracist campaign. Also noteworthy was their building of the mainly black Share Croppers Union in the South.

The above discussion of the Black Nation Thesis may suggest that the CPUSA was simply mired in modern nationalist thought. This perspective, however, would be an optical illusion that comes from solely focusing on the Black Nation Thesis, which, arguably, represents some of the CPUSA's weakest theoretical work. In general, during the Third Period (1929–35), its most revolutionary period, the CPUSA approached most matters affecting the working class from an antinationalist perspective. Moreover, notwithstanding the quasi-nationalist Black Nation Thesis, the Party's internationalist stance advanced working-class unity above all else. In short, the tension we find in the very concept of "inter-nationalism" was usually resolved by placing more emphasis on the concept's prefix.

Hence, during the Third Period, we consistently find sharp critiques of imperialist nationalism that were unparalleled at the time. The CPUSA criticized any position that supported the nationalism used by the imperialists to advance their interests. In 1931, for example, the Communist Cyril Briggs, the former leader of the African Blood Brotherhood, wrote an article for the CPUSA's *Liberator* wherein he assesses, as his title states, "The Decline of the Garvey Movement." Drawing on Lenin's writings regarding the collapse of the Second International, Briggs criticizes Garvey as imperialist in practice, since he pledged allegiance to "all flags under which he lives" (80); such patriotic loyalty is a "complete negation of the Negro liberation struggle," since it divides black workers along national lines and undermines their international struggle to defeat imperialism. The Communists' black liberation struggle, in other words, is principally internationalist, in opposition to the Garveyite "national reformists" (82). In Briggs's view, the interests of black workers *as workers* overrides the considerations of blacks workers as inhabitants of oppressed nations.

An even clearer example of the CPUSA's rejection of imperialist nationalism is James Ford's article, published in the wake of the Sixth World Congress, entitled "For the Emancipation of Negroes from Imperialism" (1929). Ford, a black Communist leader, argues that the late war awakens blacks to class consciousness and anti-imperialist struggle (9). And in a section significantly entitled "International Character of Struggle Against Imperialism," he warns against posing the "Negro Question" as primarily a racial and nationalistic issue:

> the Negroes' struggle for freedom cannot be fought upon the basis of race or nationalism solely. . . . The struggle is international, involving the unity of the Negro peoples with the exploited and oppressed of all countries.
>
> The Negro people must begin to break down all policies and tendencies that isolate them and isolate the workers and oppressed peoples of other countries from their struggles. This is of great significance since 'race war' slogans and racial issues are being raised to obscure the real struggle against imperialism. (19, emphasis added)

Ford clearly voices the danger the Communists perceived in racial and nationalistic ideologies that weaken the formation of an *international* class-consciousness. Included among the numerous nationalist movements that the CPUSA warned against were the Nationalist Movement for the Establishment of a 49th State, the Peace Movement to Liberia, and the Japanese-imperialist-sponsored Pacific Movement of the Eastern World, the latter whose slogan read: "United Front of Darker Races Under Leadership of Japan" (qtd. in Ford and Allen 19–21). Indeed, as Elizabeth Lawson succinctly states the issue in her introduction to the CPUSA's pamphlet, *The Communist Position on the Negro Question*, the overcoming of racism is "an almost perfect index of the degree of development and general class-consciousness" among the working class (1).

Since the Communists wanted to be careful not to propagate an antisocialist or proimperialist nationalism, they used the term *nationalism* cautiously. In general, during the revolutionary Third Period the Communists reserved the term to identify the nationalism promoted by the imperialists and the petit-bourgeoisie to lead workers away from class consciousness, class struggle, and class solidarity. Haywood, for instance, condemns as an instance of "Jim Crow Nationalism" the black bourgeoisie's attempts to unify blacks, while simultaneously exploiting them in their segregated residential urban districts ("The Crisis of the Jim-Crow Nationalism" 77). Olgin uses the term for black separatist movements and cautions black workers, "Do not heed your nationalist friends who try to persuade you that all whites are your enemies" (73). Not making the mistake of the Second International, the Communists during this period consistently criticized American imperialism and Americanism as grave dangers to the working class.

They thus refused to label their own position as nationalist. We see Earl Browder, the CPUSA's general secretary, finesse the issue when he disagrees with some of his comrades who believe that there are "two kinds of 'nationalism,' one bourgeois and reactionary, the other proletarian and revolutionary." On the contrary, he argues: "We are not dealing with two kinds of 'nationalism,' but with the *national liberation* struggle of the masses of the oppressed nation, on the one hand, and with the 'nationalist' system of ideas of the bourgeoisie of the oppressed nation, on the other hand, which attempts to control the national liberation movement for its own class interests" ("For National Liberation of the Negroes!" 17, emphasis added). As the above suggests, the euphemism for the CPUSA's own quasi-black-nationalist position is "national liberation." National liberation is theoretically internationalist since the liberation from imperialism unites the national liberators with other anti-imperialist and potentially socialist struggles. The Communists' anti-imperialist stance protected them from defending any nationalist movement that threatened the so-called right of national self-determination or that had imperialist designs. They were, therefore, consistently sharp critics of U.S. imperialism or its guise of Americanism. Henry George Weiss, a proletarian writer of the period, exemplifies the Communists' criticism of American nationalism in a poem he published in 1935 entitled "Americanism." Weiss sees Americanism in "God Flag Constitution / holy trinity of exploitation / signifying American legion / D.A.R. / ku klux klan / with declarations of independence / in one hand / and tar and rope in the other" (6). In short, "Americanism" is fascism with a democratic ideological cover: it promises (among other things) self-determination or "declarations of independence," while simultaneously oppressing and lynching black workers.

The relative strength of the CPUSA's critique during the first half of the decade is all the more marked when we consider the Party's subsequent and less discriminate embrace of nationalism in order to become more of a mass party during the Popular Front period (1935–39). On the issue of black nationalism, the CPUSA began to reassess Garveyism as early as 1935, with its United Front strategy of allying with all progressive, working-class organizations. In 1936, the Harlem Division of the CPUSA published a United Front pamphlet of essays by James Ford entitled *The Communists and the Struggle for Negro Liberation*. The Harlem Division's introduction urges a united front with Garveyism based on a common anti-imperialist stance, notwithstanding the long-standing Left critiques of Garvey's collusion with imperialism. The introduction employs the familiar and often shortsighted burning house analogy: Garveyites and Communists cannot quibble about their differences while Italian fascism conquers Ethiopia (6). In an address to the Harlem Division of the CPUSA, Ford, representing the Party's new position, disavows Browder's previous refusal to call the Communists' position nationalist. After speaking fondly of "some very good friendships" the CPUSA has established with U.N.I.A. (63), Ford declares, "We Negro Communists have revolutionary nationalist aims" ("Build the People's Labor Party" 66).

The United Front strategy was only the beginning of the rightward drift of the CPUSA. Beginning around 1936, the Party extended its warm welcome to any individuals or organizations that wanted to fight for "democracy" and against "fascism." Earl Browder's book, *What Is Communism?* (1936), represents the shift away from Communism to a revisionism that eventually leads, under his leadership, to the dissolution of the CPUSA in 1944 and its reemergence as the Communist Political Association, closely tied to the Democratic Party and the goal of "national unity." In the first chapter of the book, "Who Are the Americans?" Browder appeals to the "revolutionary nationalist" sentiments of the American working class in order to defend the Communists against unjust allegations that they are unpatriotic. To his credit, he steers the discussion of nationhood away from the modern criteria of race or ethnicity, and, not unlike black intellectuals had been doing for decades, he argues that nationalist identification with America is largely based on the labor one has invested in the nation (17). He refers to ethnic nationalism as "that narrow nationalism, that chauvinism, which makes a cult of a 'chosen people'" (18). For Browder, "[t]he revolutionary tradition is the heart of Americanism" (21), within which he includes the work of Patrick Henry, Tom Paine, Thomas Jefferson, as well as that of Karl Marx, Frederick Engels, Lenin, and Stalin (18–19, 22)—the assumption here being that both Jefferson and Stalin belong to the same Whitmanesque "democratic" and thus "American" tradition. The Communists, he further claims, are "the only ones who consciously continue those traditions" (21). Significantly, Browder does not once state socialism as the goal of the Communists or as explicitly linked to his vision of Americanism. Instead, he substitutes the amorphous goal of progress. Having jettisoned Marxism-Leninism, Browder gleefully proclaims, like a reformed truant, "Communism is the Americanism of the twentieth century" (21). In other words, the CPUSA's Popular Front politics essentially turned the concept of communism into a free-floating signifier that increasingly became redefined in terms of nationalist and bourgeois signifieds, such as Americanism, 1776, 1861, democracy, freedom, peace, and progress. "The figure of 'America,'" writes Michael Denning, "became a locus of ideological battles over the trajectory of US history, the meaning of race, ethnicity, and region in the United States" (129). Browder's revisionism, like that of the misleaders of the Second International, took cover under patriotism.

The Party's Americanism virtually eclipses its black nationalism. While on occasion still claiming the desirability of establishing a southern black nation, Communists appear more conscious of the implied separatism of the Black Nation Thesis and its potentially detrimental effects for their Popular Front strategy. In "The Negro People and Labor," included in What Is Communism? Browder argues that southern blacks are not ready for the revolution for self-determination and, in the meantime, the CPUSA will continue to fight for multiracial unity and economic and political reform, which will eventually lead to the revolution (144–45). Illustrating the CPUSA's increasingly patriotic stance, Browder fails entirely to raise the issue of black national self-determination in his following book, *The People's Front* (1938). In fact, in this 349-page book, he only dedicates a few paragraphs to the "Negro Question" to showcase the CPUSA's struggles for reform.

James Ford, who by 1938 was the most important black leader in the Party, having become a member of the Political Committee, the National Committee, and the New York State Committee of the CPUSA, as well as its vice-presidential candidate since 1932, also capitulates to Popular Front politics. Absent from his *The Negro and the Democratic Front* (1938) is the "national liberation" and revolutionary program of the Third Period. Instead, he constructs a revisionist American history and socialist politics, placing the democratic ideals of Washington, Jefferson, Jackson, John Brown, Lincoln, Douglass, and the CPUSA side by side. "We Communists, who are convinced that 'Communism is Twentieth Century American-ism,'" he writes, "are calling upon the people to unite more than ever for the defense of our glorious past, our present, and our still greater future" (145). Granted, *The Negro and the Democratic Front* does not banish socialism as a word and goal from its pages as does Browder's *The People's Front*; Ford defines socialism as the "true democracy" (207), and his book has the virtue of highlighting the special economic and social problems confronted by black Americans in the 1930s. However, having shelved the CPUSA's prior analysis of the capitalist economics of racism, *The Negro and the Democratic Front* remains stuck fast in reformist politics and the Com-munists' version of American nationalism.

As the above suggests, while Communists saw the problem of the twentieth century as fundamentally a class problem endemic to capital-ism, they relied too closely on Stalin and Lenin's supposedly scientific formula for nationhood. During the Popular Front the Communists made even greater ideological concessions to the postwar nationalism that was, in fact, originally promoted by the victorious powers as a foil to the Bolsheviks' growing appeal to war-weary, imperialist-weary workers. In retrospect, it is easy to see how Browder and Ford's Americanism and their belief in national unity led to a class collaborationist position that resulted in the demise of the CPUSA as an independent, Marxist-Leninist political party in 1944. After Browder's expulsion from the CPUSA, Eliza-beth Gurley Flynn, a CPUSA intellectual and organizer, regretfully told her comrades, "We are a Party based fundamentally on the working class and its struggles. The hardest thing I did and the one I can least forgive myself for was to stop talking Socialism entirely" (615). She was not alone in her regrets.

As has been well established by literary histories and studies of Depression-era proletarian literature, the CPUSA had a sizable following among writers and supported numerous left-wing journals, literary organizations, and writers' conferences. Literary theorists likewise became radicalized and produced a significant body of articles and books that provided standards of Left cultural criticism for progressive writers of the period. And since the "Negro Question" was of great importance to the CPUSA, it also reverberates through the writings of Communist literary theorists and critics. In fact, the criticism and promotion of black proletarian literature received special attention in left-wing magazines such as the *New Masses* and those produced by the many John Reed Clubs, as well as from the national Writers' Congresses held in 1935, 1937, 1939, and 1941. Black writers and intellectuals played a vital role in theorizing and putting into practice the precepts of a black Communist aesthetic.

As might be expected, the Black Nation Thesis greatly influenced the thinking of Left literary theorists about black American literature. Especially during the Third Period, most literary proletarians asserted the existence of an oppressed black nation in the South that possessed a common culture. Just as the CPUSA championed the cause of oppressed nationalities everywhere, so did literary theorists champion the black nation and particularly its culture. However, Communist critics debated about which aspects of the black national culture were progressive and usable for revolutionary struggle. As Barbara Foley notes, "some Marxist writing in the early 1930s celebrated black music and folk mythology as intrinsically oppositional . . . [although critics] . . . tended to draw the line at spirituals and other expressions of folk consciousness that did not express open resistance" (184). In particular, they privileged work songs as the finest expression of black culture. Philip Schatz, writing for the *New Masses*, went so far as to claim that: "Negro culture is perhaps the most genuine workers' culture in America" (30). Eugene Clay, a prominent black Communist theorist of the time, championed black "traditions of revolt" composed of political struggles against oppression, from slave insurrections to Reconstruction battles over land, and their "reflect[ion] in mass art forms which must be appropriated and carried onward" ("The Negro in Recent American Literature" 145–46). The belief in the revolutionary value of black working-class culture led a white Communist, Lawrence Gellert, to collect and publish southern work songs in the *New Masses* in the early 1930s and later to publish his research in a book entitled *Negro Songs of Protest* (1936).

In short, the CPUSA theorists' celebratory view of the imagined national culture of working-class blacks operated under the belief that black culture was "national in form and proletarian in content" (qtd. in Foley, 184). For them, "proletarian" signified a general class consciousness, however immanent it may be, among black workers/"peasants." "National," on the contrary, referred to black vernacular expressive forms putatively indigenous to the black nation. Like their Communist counterparts, these critics perceived a unity between class and national concerns in black culture.

However, there were dissenting voices that saw little of value even in the vernacular tradition and the work songs. That is to say, Communist cultural theorists were not all of one mind, which is not surprising since they were attempting to theorize black culture in radically new ways. The black Communist critic Eugene Gordon, in his address to the first American Writers' Congress in 1935, dismisses folk and work songs as expressive of a stunted black national psychology and culture. He maintains that, even though southern blacks comprise a nation, they were "a slave nation. Natural vents to national aspirations were clogged up. The result was a national psychosis" (143). For Gordon, political and economic oppression bred cultural repression, which resulted in the "futile protests" of the folk tales, spirituals, hymns, and work songs. And since the national culture is "psychotic," modern black writers, whom he characterizes as petty bourgeois, remain trapped in a tradition of futile protest. Therefore, while in disagreement with Schatz and Clay on the value of historical black culture, he was nonetheless committed to fostering a black national culture expressive of working-class life (145).

Most theorists of black literature shared the assumption that the black national workers' culture must be authentic. They feared bourgeois values could dislodge the black national form from the working-class content. And it is none other than the Harlem Renaissance that they point to as a warning to radical black writers. Schatz writes in 1930:

In the past five years there have been a dozen dramas and musical come-
dies either dealing with Negro life or employing Negroes in important
parts. There have been "all-colored revues." The talkies, catching Holly-
wood hard-up for material [sic] have forced the white producers to use
Negro talent and Negro subjects. "Negro culture" is being encouraged
on a wholesale scale, and idle, muddled minds have seized on it as new
fad.

And while the bodies remain black, the work of the Negro artists is
being bleached of all the realness, sincerity and vitality of art which has
its roots in life. (8)

Clay and Gordon also dismiss the Harlem Renaissance as a self-serving
market-produced fad without proletarian content. For Clay, black writers
succumbed to the triumphant, postwar American bourgeoisie that
"wanted new amusements and new thrills . . . and began to fawn upon
and lionize the 'new Negro'" ("The Negro in Recent American Literature" 146). And, as early as 1928, William Patterson, a black Communist
who saw some value in a few of the aesthetic and political accomplishments of the Harlem Renaissance, expresses perhaps the sharpest words
on the subject when he writes that black poets "voice the aspirations of a
rising petty bourgeoisie . . . They are sensationalists, flirting with popularity and huge royalties. They are cowards" ("Awake Negro Poets!" 10). A
truly authentic black national culture must remain firmly working class.

For black writing produced during the revolutionary 1930s, critics
were even more demanding. Third Period critics assert that new black
writing should be "national in form and *socialist* in content" (Filatova 107,
emphasis added). Unlike the work songs of the past, socialist literature
and art should not reproduce the ideological representations of black
workers as simply passive victims who suffer their capitalist exploitation
with Christian humility. This perspective informed the Communists' rejection of the spirituals, as well as Anne Elistratova's early (1931) critical
evaluation of the *New Masses*'s handling of the "Negro Question." Elistratova condemns the undialectical drawing entitled "Southern Holiday" by
Mitchel Siporin that depicts "the lynching of a Negro in mystical tones,
something like a Walpurgis night, while the figure of the lynched Negro,
as though crucified, is illuminated by [sic] mysterious 'sacred' halo. These
utterly non-revolutionary motifs, decadent by their nature, find their
analogy in a certain section of the literary output of the journal" (111).

Elistratova goes on to single out, and perhaps somewhat unfairly, Langston Hughes's "Tired" (1931) as a decadent poem with a passive mood. The poem speaks of being "tired of waiting . . . / For the world to become good / And beautiful and kind." Yet, like Siporin's drawing, one can recognize that Hughes's poem may mystify class struggle by alluding to the bourgeoisie as "worms . . . eating / At the rind" of the world and by presenting class struggle as taking "a knife / And cut[ting] the world in two" to "see what worms are eating / At the rind." Conversely, the criterion for socialist content finds positive expression in Clay's praise for some of the more agitational literary work of Langston Hughes, Richard Wright, and Sterling Brown. Hughes expresses the requisite revolutionary attitude for black proletarian writing when he tells writers at the first Writers' Congress that they need "seek to unite blacks and whites . . . on the solid ground of daily working-class struggle to wipe out, now and forever, all the old inequalities of the past" (139).

The revolutionary criteria for evaluating black art during the Third Period fell victim to the political opportunism of the Popular Front. Perhaps expectedly, as the decade wore on and the CPUSA become more and more immersed in reformist politics and Americanism, literary theorists (following Browder, Ford, and other Communist leaders), increasingly downplayed the Black Nation Thesis. The formula that black writing should be "national in form and socialist in content" was watered down to mean that it should be "American" in form and "democratic" in content. Like other political expression, it should be for "the people" (7), as Mike Gold writes in his introduction to Langston Hughes's Popular Front pamphlet of poems, A New Song (1938). Barbara Foley aptly concludes, "In a curious political inversion, the distinctive cultural expressions of the black 'oppressed nation,' originally held to be inherently antagonistic to capitalist and neo-feudalist oppression, were assimilated to a 'left' American nationalism that, as the decade progressed, became increasingly difficult to distinguish from garden-variety American patriotism" (192). In fact, the CPUSA's previous privileging of and researches on black folk culture provided rich resources for their Popular Front nationalism. Black "traditions of revolt" became "American" traditions of revolt, since, in effect, blacks were now construed as a segment of "the people." Popular Front ideology transformed the "slave insurrections to Reconstruction battles" Clay praises into great moments of a uniquely American history.

Furthermore, during the Popular Front the Communists' definition of progressive black culture was more expansive than during the Third Period. They perceived jazz, the blues, and spirituals as existing on an equal plane. During the Popular Front, the New Masses favorably covered black musical events and recordings. For example, it ran full-page ads of a performance at Carnegie Hall on December 24, 1939, From Spirituals to Swing, which featured Benny Goodman and Count Basie, including other popular musicians such as Pete Johnson, Big Bill Broonzy, and Ida Cox. Sterling Brown, a Communist fellow traveler at the time, was the emcee for the event billed as "A Rare Event of Blues, Boogie-Woogie Piano, Spirituals and Swing" (New Masses, Dec. 19, 1939, 27). Two days after the performance, the New Masses ran a rave review of the performance and of a recording of similar music produced the previous year. Absent from the article is any discussion of the politics of the music or of issues of class and work. It is also interesting to note that some of the ads for the show feature an African mask in the center of the page, thus suggesting the "African" identity of the music and further erasing issues of class. Indeed, the tie between the New Masses and jazz was even closer than the ad and review may suggest, since, as Michael Denning tells us, "Eric Bernay, the business manager of the New Masses, also had a record store, The Music Room, and founded Keynote Records in 1940. Keynote specialized in jazz and folk music and issued a variety of Popular Front recordings" (338). It appears that the literary Left had returned to the kind of dual nationalism that characterized the Harlem Renaissance and Locke's New Negro anthology, the latter which also included photographs of African masks. Thus, by the decade's end, Langston Hughes, once as revolutionary as any Third Period writer, could write with Popular Front conviction that, "We are all Americans. We want to create the American dream, a finer and more democratic America" ("The Negro Troops" 62).

It is difficult not to conclude that the CPUSA's and literary proletarians' construction and/or support of national identifications, particularly during the Popular Front, are deeply indebted to a history of bourgeois nationalist discourse. In their attempt to be a mass political party in an era of nation-states, the Communists made concessions to the ways that the working class had been taught to conceive of itself in nationalistic ways. As Eric Hobsbawm colorfully puts it, the Communists wanted "to refuse the devil's armies the monopoly of the best marching tunes" (*Nations and Nationalism* 145). Nonetheless, the CPUSA made available to black and white writers a range of powerful, if contradictory, critiques of nationalism, racism, and imperialism that they adapted to their own politically charged literary pursuits.

5

Langston Hughes's Radical Poetry and the "End of Race"

"The voice of the red world / Is our voice, too."

Langston Hughes, *Scottsboro Limited*

For a number of reasons, Langston Hughes's radical poetry, the bulk of which he wrote between 1932 and 1938, has received little scholarly attention and has yet to make its way into many anthologies of African American and American literature (with the notable exception of a few poems in the vanguard *The Heath Anthology of American Literature*). The origins of this benign and not-so-benign neglect lie in Hughes's own retrospective ambivalence toward his earlier radical activities and poetry. As early as 1940 he substantially repressed the memory of his involvement with the proletarian literary movement in his autobiography, *The Big Sea*. And we can surmise that the hostile recovery of this memory by none other than the House Un-American Activities Committee in the 1950s did little to encourage Hughes to include his explicitly "red" poetry in his *Selected Poems* (1959). But Hughes's repression of his radical poetry in the 1940s and 1950s was only one symptom of a debilitating neurosis in American society: the Cold War fear of the radical "other," and that even deeper fear of one's own "un-American" impulses. Of course, writers rarely exercise power over the public reception of their work, and Hughes was no exception. The exclusion of proletarian literature from academic canons was in large part a New Critical achievement; 1930s radical poetry was not considered poetry at all, since it was not—nor ever aimed to be—autotelic. With a few exceptions, and notably James Smethurst's *The New Red Negro: The Literary Left and African American Poetry, 1930–1946*, what limited scholarship has been generated about Hughes's poetry tends to dismiss the works of this period because they do not measure up to aesthetic standards or because they fail to express an essential black identity. After all, they embrace a Communist perspective critical of the black nationalist or Pan-Africanist ideology attributed to his earlier Harlem Renaissance poems.

The neglect of Hughes's radical poetry is unfortunate. He ought to be considered one of the first American poets effectively to challenge the post-World War I ethnic nationalism that informed much of the politics and literature of the Harlem Renaissance, including some of his own early blues poetry, as well as that which fueled European fascism. Hughes's internationalist poetry aims dialectically to transcend the categories of race and nation in order to overcome the fragmentation of global working-class struggles. This effort may not have produced what some critics would deem formally beautiful or racially expressive poetry, but if Hughes chose to forgo some of his earlier accomplishments for politics, it was not because the two are mutually exclusive but because the black vernacular aesthetic of his early poems implied a nationalist politics he could no longer accept. Ironically, then, Hughes's work during the 1930s speaks directly to those who would dismiss it, challenging scholars of black literature and culture to look more critically at black nationalist literary aesthetics and politics, and prodding us, perhaps, to rethink the historical relationships between poetics and politics.

While scholars still debate how to periodize the Harlem Renaissance—that is, whether it ended in 1929 or 1940—it is clear that during the Great Depression, the Harlem Renaissance's dream of equality achieved through cultural production "crashed," along with many other hopes of economic and political progress in America. The emergent political mobility of large masses of workers changed the political landscape of the country by throwing into question the postwar view popular among disillusioned intellectuals of a history devoid of active proletarian agency. Indeed, in the mid 1920s, when the American Left was at its transitional weak point, somewhere between postwar Socialism and depression-era Communism, Floyd Dell had already sounded the alarm on his contemporaries for capitulating to the new political and historical problems that confronted the working class. "Facing an ironic doom which it feels powerless to avert, the intelligentsia of our time," wrote Dell, "has for the most part put aside with a kind of shame its broken and shattered ideals . . . [and] . . . have retired into a sort of new Ivory Tower hastily jerry-built according to some fantastic futurist blue-print" (241). While Hughes never created "fantastic futurist blue-prints," he certainly shared with many of his contemporaries political passivity usually suggestive of demoralization. In the 1930s, however, the Communist Party of the United States (CPUSA) became a focal point of interest for Hughes, because he saw the CPUSA as an organization with an explicitly antiracist and democratic program that could organize the stirring masses. As Hughes wrote in 1932, "If the Communists don't awaken the Negro of the South, who will?" (qtd. in Berry 142). His later renunciation of Communism in the 1940s and 1950s and his insistence that he was never a member of the CPUSA are of little consequence here when we consider the depth of his support for Communism and its influence on his work in the 1930s. Hughes's experience in the 1930s forced him to rethink race, politics, and aesthetics.

Hughes's move to the left was in large part a recognition of the limitations of a cultural nationalist perspective of social relations. We can assume that witnessing the millions of white workers unemployed and underemployed made it difficult to continue to believe that the "white man" was master of his own fate, let alone that of black Americans. In the 1930s, the working class was publicly amassing—whether in breadlines, marches, or strikes—to an unprecedented degree. "[T]he external facts of the Depression," writes James Hart, "remained visible to all in stockmarket statistics, boarded-up factories, apple vendors, and breadlines" (249). In *The Big Sea*, Hughes vividly depicts this experience of the Depression around 1930, when he was about to quit the rich white patron, Charlotte Mason, who had supported him from 1927 to 1930. He writes: "New York began to be not so pleasant that winter. People were sleeping in subways or on newspapers in office doors, because they had no homes. I got so I didn't like to go to dinner on luxurious Park Avenue [with his patron]—and come out and see people hungry on the streets, huddled in subway entrances all night and filling Manhattan Transfer like a flop house. I knew I could very easily and quickly be there, too" (319–20).

Perhaps Hughes would not have quit his patron as soon as he did if not confronted with the visible contradiction between New York's multiracial homeless and jobless and Park Avenue's wealthy white elite. In any case, we know that Hughes decided to break with Mason because she wanted to prevent him from writing about the issue that the depression threw into relief: class inequality. Not surprisingly, one of the culminating events in his break with Mason was his publication of "Advertisement for the Waldorf-Astoria" (1931), which satirizes an advertisement for the opening of the luxurious hotel in 1931. "So when you've got no place to go, homeless and hungry ones," Hughes writes, "choose the Waldorf as a background for your rags" (144).

Yet, the shock of the depression (especially the recognition of mass multiracial unemployment) was not itself the determining factor in Hughes's move away from nationalism. Hughes's politicization is more closely linked to the CPUSA's revolutionary Third Period politics (1929–35) that informed the proletarian literary movement to which he belonged. Of great importance here is the Sixth World Congress of the Communist International (Comintern) held in 1928 that galvanized the American Communist Party, as well as other parties in the International, into a Bolshevik party that fought for both reform and revolution. It was also at the Sixth World Congress that the Communists decided that the Stalinist-Leninist arguments about oppressed nationalities apply to black Americans. Of the two tendencies within the Comintern's political program from the 1930s concerning African Americans—that is, a quasi-nationalistic view of African American identity, oppression, and emancipation, and an antiracist, internationalist perspective—it is the latter tendency that Hughes chose to incorporate into his literary practice. Hughes, interestingly, can be said to have been left of the CP on the issues of race and nationality. One should note that, while it is difficult to take seriously many of Hughes's statements during the McCarthy period concerning his involvement in the Communist movement, Hughes's proletarian writings support his claim in the 1950s that he was not persuaded by "the Communist theory of a Negro state for the Black Belt" ("Langston Hughes Speaks" 158).

Hughes's radical perspective is most apparent in his analysis of black oppression in the United States. By 1932, he clearly was moving away from his nationalist perspective as a Harlem Renaissance writer and toward a view of class rather than race as the basis for both economic racism and collective struggle. In *Scottsboro Limited* (1932), for example, an agit-prop verse play about the Scottsboro case, Hughes represents the accused young men in the process of becoming politically astute. While "hoboing" on a train in search of work prior to their arrest, the nameless and emblematic black young men realize the class basis of their wage slavery and thus their class affinity with white workers:

> 6th Boy: (*In wonder*) *Look a-yonder you-all, at dem fields*
> *Burstin' wid de crops they yields.*
> *Who gets it all?*
> 3rd Boy: *White folks.*
> 8th Boy: *You mean de rich white folks.*
> 2nd Boy: *Yes, 'cause de rich ones owns de land.*
> *And they don't care nothin' 'bout de po' white man.*
> 3rd Boy: *You's right. Crackers is just like me—*
> *Po' whites and niggers, ain't neither one free.*

A characteristic Hughesian discursive strategy here is the dramatization of the movement from a nationalist to a postnationalist consciousness and self-identification. In fact, in his radical poetry, he consistently replaces the "black, like me" self-identification of his Harlem Renaissance period with a class-conscious sentiment that might be paraphrased "worker, like me." In "Air Raid Over Harlem" (1935), for example, he ends the poem with a call to workers' multiracial unity: "Black and white workers united as one . . . THE BLACK AND WHITE WORKERS— / you and me" (188).

A glaring example of Hughes's critique of a nationalist consciousness occurs in his rather antiaesthetic poem entitled "White Man," which begins with a black nationalist persona who comments on how the "white man" has exploited blacks economically by confining them to low-paying, devalued jobs as garbage men and janitors; imperialistically by colonizing Africa; and culturally by signing black jazz musicians to record companies that garnish the profits. Yet, two-thirds of the way into the poem, we find a discursive strategy similar to that of *Scottsboro Limited* when Hughes's persona comes around to asking a postnationalist rhetorical question: "Is it true, White Man? / Is your name in a book / Called the *Communist Manifesto?* / Is your name spelled / C-A-P-I-T-A-L-I-S-T? / Are you always a White Man? / Huh?" (194–95). It is difficult to know what capitalists of color Hughes had in mind when he typed those words, but it is conceivable he could have been referring to those "champions of the darker races," as the Japanese imperialists represented themselves, or perhaps the small black American bourgeoisie who, as one CP pamphlet at that time explained, "makes its profits by taking advantage of segregation and the ideas of 'white superiority' . . . by speculating in real estate in the segregated sections of large cities and by extracting extremely high rents from their Negro tenants . . . [or in the cosmetic industry] by commercializing the idea of 'white beauty'" (Ford and Allen 8). Nonetheless, Hughes's radical poetry shatters from "below" the myth of exclusively white domination by depicting the existence of a poor white working class exploited in common with blacks, and from "above" by representing the existence of a black bourgeoisie exploiting in common with wealthy whites. Consequently, he fosters multiracial working-class unity and militant action against ruling classes of any color. In "Open Letter to the South"—originally published as "Red Flag over Tuskegee" in 1932—he plainly rejects the Booker T. Washington-Supreme Court "separate as the fingers" segregationist ideology and, instead, urges union between black and white workers. Perhaps his strongest image for his rejection of black cultural nationalism and embracing of Communism is none other than that of "Tuskegee with a new [red] flag on the tower!" (161).

But it is not as if Hughes's class consciousness made him oblivious to the importance of race in America and around the world. Independently of the Communists' position on the "Negro Question," he knew well that black workers are subject to special forms of oppression under capitalism such as segregation, racist violence, and super-exploitation. Yet, to quote a title of a speech he addressed to the Second International Writers' Congress in 1937, he did not want to make "too much of race." He believed too much has been made of race, because even the ruling classes will overlook the racial antagonisms they created in the first place if they need people of color for cannon fodder or cheap labor: "The same Fascists who forced Italian peasants to fight in Africa now force African Moors to fight in Europe . . . Japan attempts to force the Chinese of Manchuria to work and fight under Japanese supervision for the glory and wealth of the Tokyo bourgeoisie—one colored people dominating another at the point of guns. Race means nothing when it can be turned to Fascist use" (103). Hughes witnessed the ways in which race is manufactured for devastating nationalist ends. Franco and the Spanish fascists, for instance, mobilized African Moors under the banner of "Viva España." In "Letter from Spain" (1937), a poem Hughes wrote while visiting war-torn Spain, he captures the tragic irony of a Moroccan soldier fighting for Spanish fascists when, in the voice of a black American International Brigade soldier, he writes: "We captured a wounded Moor today. / He was just as dark as me. / I said, Boy, what you been doin' here / Fighting against the free?" (201). Race, or what Etienne Balibar calls that "fictive ethnicity around which [nationalism] is organized" (49), is clearly illusory for Hughes. "We Negroes of America," Hughes writes, "are tired of a world divided superficially on the basis of blood and color, but in reality on the basis of poverty and power—the rich over the poor, no matter what their color" (102). Like others in the CP, Hughes views the Spanish Civil War as one of "Class Against Class." Conversely, because race is a fluid concept without scientific validation, it is an important issue for Hughes: fascists manipulate the concept to "hurt and impede the rising power of the working class" through the old familiar strategy of divide and conquer. It is fair to say that the purpose of Hughes's radical poetry is to explode pseudo-scientific theories of racial difference among the working class in order, ultimately, to abolish the socioeconomic system that propagates and thrives on racism. But it is through a double strategy of *recognition* of the consequences of the concept of race and a *rejection* of race as an a priori category that Hughes struggles for internationalism. It is for this reason that he concludes his speech by stating how he and other progressive black writers and activists "represent the end of race": internationalism represents a dialectical model that must recognize a world artificially and devastatingly divided by race as a way of conceptually and, eventually, materially, negating the concept of race altogether. "Fascists know that when there is no more race," Hughes states, "there will be no more capitalism, and no more war, and no more money for the munition makers, because the workers of the world will have triumphed" (104).

Hughes's provocative claim to represent the end of race is borne out powerfully in "Always the Same," published five years earlier in the *Liberator*. The poem presents a panoramic view of the global exploitation of blacks by the finance capital of major imperialists. Irrespective of locale,

whether in Harlem, Haiti, Central America, or Tripoli, to be black is to
be: "Exploited, beaten, and robbed, / Shot and killed / . . . / For the
wealth of the exploiters" (165). The binary Hughes sets up between
white imperialists and people of color has the potential to be interpreted
according to a nationalist politics, but Hughes undermines a nationalist
take on the exploitation by suggesting that, instead of residing in any of
these besieged black locales and fighting for national self-determination,
he is driven away from "all the black lands everywhere" (165). No longer
feeling himself to be a Harlem Renaissance "exile" from an idealized
Africa, Hughes would rather "deracinate" himself (my word) by having
his blood—that pseudo-scientific race marker—make "one with the
blood / Of all the struggling workers in the world" (165). In other
words, here operates the figure of class blood that serves to disperse
Hughes across national/racial boundaries. And, specifically, it is the notion of the "blood-red flag" of Communism that unifies the world's
workers whose faces are "black, white, olive, yellow, brown" (166).

The poem also clearly illustrates anti-imperialism, which, as I argued
in chapter 4, was one of the hallmarks of the CP and the work of proletarian writers. During the revolutionary Third Period, Communists linked
anti-imperialism to antinationalism, or, more precisely, they consistently
criticized the nationalism of oppressor nations and viewed "national liberation" movements as inherently anti-imperialist. In agreement with his
comrades, Hughes wrote a number of poems that demonstrate the
breadth of his sympathy for workers of all colors and nationalities who
were the subjects of imperialism. Like "The Same," these poems avoid
any kind of nationalistic siding: American, English, French, Spanish, Japanese, and Italian imperialists and fascists are part of one and the same
oppressive class for Hughes.

His first anti-imperialist poem of the 1930s is "Merry Christmas"
(1930), published in the Christmas issue of the New Masses. The poem is
written in the ironic mode, juxtaposing Christmas greetings with murder-
ous actions by imperialists. The first stanza proclaims: "Merry Christmas,
China, / From the gun-boats in the river, / Ten-inch shells for Christmas
gifts, / And peace on earth forever" (132). The following two stanzas
indict English imperialism in India and the long "murder and rape" of
Africa. Hughes is particularly critical of U.S. imperialism, since he devotes
two stanzas (four and five) to its domination in the Caribbean:

Ring Merry Christmas, Haiti!
(And drown the voodoo drums—
We'll rob you to the Christmas hymns
Until the next Christmas comes.)

Ring Merry Christmas, Cuba!
(While Yankee domination
Keeps a nice fat president
In a little half-starved nation.) (132)

Hughes alludes in these lines to the history of attempts of imperialists, from the colonial Spanish to the U.S. armed forces, to stamp out the African culture (such as voodoo) brought over to the West Indies by African slaves, a history that his otherwise progressive *New Masses* readership may have not known. Hughes takes on "Yankee domination" in the Caribbean, and, by implication, the religious and political ideologies that justified the domination. Aside from his obvious criticism of the Christian camouflage for colonialization, he also invokes the imperialist Monroe Doctrine that authorized U.S. intervention in the hemisphere for reasons of "national interests." Hughes suggests the hypocrisy of such "national interests," since by the 1920s U.S. companies owned two-thirds of Cuba's farmland, thanks in large part to President Gerado Machado y Morales (the "nice fat president") whose reign, as a CPUSA pamphlet published a few years after Hughes's poem states,

> was one of stark terror; of outlawing workers' organizations; of crushing strikes; of jailing workers' leaders and throwing many of them to the sharks in Havana Bay; of increasingly heavy taxation on the necessities of life . . . And for eight long years, Machado was the favored son of Wall Street; he paid interest on loans . . . American imperialism, American banks and industrialists, are responsible for the misery of the Cuban people, for the murder of workers, peasants and students. (Simons 9–10)

Similarly, between 1915 and 1934, the U.S. Marines occupied Haiti and established control over customs houses and port authorities. They also created the Haitian National Guard, which, along with the Marines, forced peasants into corvée labor that built roads necessary for the exploitative commerce of the Caribbean country. Hughes packs into this short poem his sympathy early on in the depression for communist anti-imperialism.

As the decade progressed, Hughes also wrote anti-imperialist poems in support of the Spanish Republicans during the Civil War ("Song of Spain," "Letter from Spain," "Postcard from Spain," "Air Raid: Barcelona"); poems in support of Ethiopia during the Italian fascist invasion and occupation ("Call of Ethiopia," "Broadcast on Ethiopia"); and poems in support of a beleaguered China by Japanese forces and Czechoslovakia by the Nazis ("Roar China," "Song for Ourselves"). He was appalled at the atrocities that the imperialist states were committing around the world. But, again, it is important to emphasize the precise political context that helped to shape his anti-imperialist poetry. The Communist International had warned in the early 1930s of the danger of fascism to the world's workers. At the Seventh World Congress of the Communists International in 1935, one of its members insightfully declared: "The adventurist plans of the German fascists are very far-reaching and count on a war of revenge against France, dismemberment of Czechoslovakia, annexation of Austria, destruction of the independence of the Baltic states" (qtd. in *Communist International* 878). The Comintern also knew that France and England could not be counted on to confront Nazism. Comintern theorists reasoned that these capitalist states may conspire with the Nazis in order to weaken each other, or to avoid attack by the Nazis, or else to lend support to the Nazis when they moved eastward in an attempt to destroy their common enemy, the Soviet Union. In fact, both Britain's Neville Chamberlain and France's Edouard Daladier aided Hitler's invasion and annexation of a portion of Czechoslovakia (the Sudeten districts) in September of 1938 by convincing the Czech government to comply with Hitler's dictate. On cover after cover and in article after article, the Comintern's theoretical organ, *The Communist International*, drew attention to the predatory aims of the imperialists and the need for a united front and, later, a popular front against war and fascism. And, significantly, the Comintern stressed that what may appear as regional political problems had, in fact, global implications. In an article detailing the treachery of the French and English governments over the issue of Czechoslovakia, the editors of *The Communist International* warned: "The fate of the Czechoslovakian workers and peasants fleeing in thousands before the bayonets of the German and Polish army of occupation, leaving their homes, their cattle and their belongings in the hands of the robbers, should warn the workers of all countries of the fate which threatens them if they yield to the fascist butchers" ("The Conspiracy of Munich" 882). The Comintern took the same position on the Italian-German-Spanish fascist axis that eventually defeated the Spanish Loyalists as well as on the Japanese invasion of China. Since the magazine was widely distributed among the members and friends of the CPUSA, Hughes most likely had read this or similar passages that provided an internationalist perspective of world events for him.

"Song for Ourselves," one of the last poems Hughes wrote during the 1930s, illustrates his development as a Communist poet deeply concerned with workers' lives, irrespective of their skin color or nationality, in an increasingly fascistic world. The poem, published in September of 1938, reacts to news of the fall of Czechoslovakia:

> Czechoslovakia lynched on a swastika cross!
>   Blow, bitter winds, blow!
>   Blow, bitter winds, blow!
> Nails in her hands and nails in her feet,
>   Left to die slow!
>   Left to die slow!
> Czechoslovakia! Ethiopia! Spain!
>   One after another!
>   One after another!
> Where will the long snake of greed strike again?
>   Will it be here, brother? (207)

Hughes begins the poem by suggestively drawing a parallel between a "lynched" Czechoslovakia and thousands of lynched black Americans. He expands the historical meaning of lynching for his American readers and thus suggests that both black Americans' and the Czechoslovakians' sufferings are not isolated—not regional—but interconnected. Hughes may be drawing on the popular equation made by black Communists that the Nazis were not all that different from southern landowners and politicians; both Czechoslovakians and blacks were victimized by a common, racist oppressor that conceived of itself as a master race. His conflation of lynching with crucifixion also connects the conquered Czechoslovakians with the familiar trope of the Black Christ found in numerous African American texts, including Hughes's own "Christ in Alabama" (1931). The Czech Christ has also been betrayed, but here by the English and French ruling classes that leave her "to die slow," even though all parties belonged to the League of Nations, which was designed to check such aggressions following World War I. Not content with simply establishing these connections, Hughes then links the Czechoslovakians' fate with that of other peoples overrun by imperialist fascism (the Ethiopians and the Spanish), and attempts to make the issue crucially important in America by directly addressing his reader, and to boot, as "brother." It is also important that he published the poem in the New York Post, thereby reaching out to a more conservative and mass audience than if he had published it in the New Masses or Opportunity. This antinationalist or internationalist poem represents just how much Hughes's political sensibilities had grown in a decade.

Hughes's dialectical view of race and nation, however, carries within it the problem of accepting the notion that nations (as defined by the possession of a common cultural identity), if not races, exist. Like his Soviet and American Communist counterparts, he simultaneously recognizes non-race-based national and class determinations of working-class identity. His radical poetry works to situate national identities within international class coordinates. Thus, he concludes "Good Morning, Revolution" (1932) by imagining the "signing" of the first radio broadcast from Soviet America to the world's workers: "And we'll sign it: Germany / Sign it: China / Sign it: Africa / Sign it: Poland / Sign it: Italy / Sign it: America." And then, significantly, "Sign it with my one name: Worker" (163). For Hughes, in short, workers have nationalities, but they are less important than their class positioning and interests.

This vestige of nationalism in otherwise radical thought becomes particularly important in the poetry Hughes wrote during the Popular Front period (1935–39), whose quintessential formulation, as discussed in the previous chapter, was that of Earl Browder, general secretary of the CPUSA, who claimed that "Communism is Twentieth Century Americanism" (The People's Front 269). That is, in the American context, the relatively critical notion of nationality in the Third Period fell prey to the powerful current of nationalism in the dominant American culture. The Popular Front rhetoric of the American Communist Party at points becomes virtually unrecognizable from mainstream American nationalist discourse. As early as 1936, Browder also stated in a radio interview that the CPUSA had "no different definition of revolution than that given to us by Thomas Jefferson" (199), which, needless to say, is a misreading of both Jefferson and the classic texts of Marxism-Leninism. Hughes never became an unquestioning patriot of America—he knew firsthand the hypocrisy of what he termed "the old My-Country-'Tis-of-Thee lie" ("To Negro Writers" 140)—but, during the Popular Front, he did somewhat uncritically embrace American nationalism. A prime example is his "Let America Be America Again" (1938), a lament for the failure of the "American dream" and a plea for a truly democratic and egalitarian America. The point of the poem is relatively simple: the democratic and egalitarian ideal of America does not and has never existed in practice because of class inequality, because of "those who live like leeches on the people's lives" (191). The poem is highly ironic since the title and refrain—"let America be America again"—is undermined in the poem by the absence of a preexistent manifestly ideal America. In Hughes's characteristically multiracial perspective, the dispossessed include Native Americans, working-class European immigrants, and blacks.

Hughes participates in the myth-making processes of a rather popular version of American nationalism: the true America of the future will embody Jeffersonian political ideals: it will be a nation of, by, and for "the people," based on the notion of inalienable rights and freedom from tyranny. America signifies the constitution of a free and democratic society. Granted, the poem does not contain the central myth-making components of the postwar ethnic nationalism. Nonetheless, Hughes's poem (re)creates a cultural fiction of a nation. Significantly absent from Hughes's reconstruction of the American past is a recognition that this land was colonized in the first place, and not simply for abstract political concepts by "the one who dreamt our basic dream / In that Old World while still a serf of kings" (190). While he does recognize "the red man driven from the land," he confusingly situates the Native American as one of the people's chorus who wants "America [to] be America again." And what particularly brings the poem into conflict with his earlier internationalism is its exclusive focus on a national, and not international, "people's" identity. The publication of "Let America" signifies that by 1938 Hughes, influenced by Popular Front politics (which, aside from advocating a "people's" nationalism, no longer advocated socialist revolution and the class-based politics of the Third Period) was moving away from his radical beliefs; nonetheless, even then he was still capable of writing a good anti-imperialist poem like "Song for Ourselves."

Interestingly, between 1932 and 1938, Hughes rarely draws on African American expressive forms, which may appear peculiar considering that a large part of his fame in the 1920s rests on his poetic appropriation of such forms. In fact, after 1931, with his publication of *The Negro Mother and Other Dramatic Recitations* as well as "Sylvester's Dying Bed," Hughes rarely wrote blues poetry. And in *The Negro Mother*, he only suggests the use of the blues, jazz, and spirituals to accompany the recitations of "Broke," "The Black Clown," and "The Negro Mother," otherwise conventional poems. The only mid 1930s poem he wrote loosely on the blues form is "Death in Harlem" (1935). Not until 1937 does Hughes write a complete poem in black vernacular ("Sister Johnson Marches"); and only in 1939, after what I have been calling his radical phase, does he return to his Renaissance style by publishing six blues poems in a year's time, among them "Six-Bits Blues," "Red Clay Blues" (with Richard Wright), and "Hey-Hey Blues."

While he did not explain his rationale for virtually abandoning African American expressive forms—another aporia of this little known "red" Hughes—we can surmise that he no longer believed that they were appropriate vehicles for the content of his ideas. We can surmise that he viewed them as limited in two fundamental ways. On the one hand, as evident in "The Negro Artist," for Hughes, African American expressive forms expressed a common African American subjectivity that constituted black community. In an attempt to distance himself from 1920s-style nationalistic theories of black cultural forms, Hughes shies away from national aesthetic forms that could not adequately express the subjectivity of the white worker as well. His disuse of such forms also suggests a rejection of the CP's own nationalization of culture. On the other hand, for Hughes and other Third Period Communists, the use of blues and spirituals in the 1920s did not express (at least explicitly) militant politics against oppression. As stated earlier, a weariness bred of a sense of hopelessness about oppression infuses Hughes's blues poetry. In the 1920s, he expresses his protest against the life-negating racism of America through a longing for mythic racial origins and identity or in culturally affirmative activities such as African American dance and song. The multiracial solidarity and militancy that Hughes experienced in the 1930s could not be adequately expressed by the nationalism, despondency, loneliness, or even the cultural rebelliousness associated with these forms. In short, he views the collective optimism that imbued the proletarian movement as incongruous with the blues. He hints at this notion when he commented in 1933: "The time has passed for us to sit by and bemoan our fate. We need now an art and a literature which will arouse us to our fate. Already we have had too much literature in the vein of the spirituals, lamenting our fate and bemoaning our condition, but suggesting no remedy except humbleness and docility" (qtd. in Berry 183). The proletarian play *Stevedore* (1934) by Paul Peters and George Sklar dramatizes this militant rejection of the blues for proletarian political struggle when the protagonist, a black longshoreman who struggles with his black coworkers to unite with the white workers and fight for their labor and human rights, shuts off a blues-playing radio before he begins to argue for the necessity of struggle (24). It is no wonder that most of Hughes's Communist poetry is agit-prop, interested in politicizing and mobilizing his readers for militant struggle against racism and capitalism. This is not to suggest that Hughes's (or Peters's and Sklar's) radical view of the blues is the correct, let alone the only, cultural interpretation of the blues. Theories of the blues abound; they have been interpreted as expressions of self-pity, celebration, protest, and so forth (Tracy). My purpose is merely to explain Hughes's own changing political relationship to the blues in the 1930s.

The language Hughes does use in the 1930s can be characterized as a working-class vernacular he believed had multiracial mass appeal. His diction has much in common with that of Carl Sandburg, who was one of his early literary influences. Hughes's poetic language is informal, often intimate, not unlike speech one might hear between friends. It is devoid of philosophical or political abstraction, like much proletarian poetry, in order to appeal to the average worker unschooled in Marxist theory. In "Good Morning, Revolution" (1932), for example, he apostrophizes revolution as a new "buddy": "Listen, Revolution, / We're buddies, see— / Together, / We can take everything / . . . And turn 'em over to the people who work. / Rule and run 'em for us people who work" (163). In "Open Letter to the South" (1938), his poetry displays the mainstream masculinist bias of much proletarian literature in an attempt to speak "straight"

to southern white, male workers. Referring to the southern worker as a
"brother," Hughes concludes in a gentlemanly manner: "White
worker, / Here is my hand. / Today, We're Man to Man" (161). And, as
James Smethurst recently argues, Hughes's use (rare, I should add) of
standard poetic diction to represent the southern black workers' voice in
Scottsboro Limited is at odds with his work from the 1920s and 1940s, as
well as with the CPUSA's cultural criteria of black nationhood. Indeed,
the Scottsboro "boys" do not seem to share national characteristics, thus
also supporting the notion that Hughes at least in part disagreed with the
Black Nation Thesis (105).

A significant portion of Hughes's radical poetry is also intended to be
performative. In order to bridge the gap between art and the working
class that inheres under capitalism, he wrote mass songs, recitations, short
plays, and poetic sketches to be performed by and for multiracial workers.
Hughes's A New Song (1938), a pamphlet of poems published by the International Workers Order, includes two chants, two ballads, three songs,
and a number of other free verse poems. His "Chant for May Day" clearly
illustrates his intention to appeal to the working class. In a prefatory note
to the chant, he writes, "To be read by a Workman with, for background,
the rhythmic waves of rising and re-rising Mass Voices" (209). The
"Mass-Voices," ten voices at the poem's beginning and from sixty to one
hundred at its end, declare multiracial, working-class solidarity and swear
to "Take Power" (210). In this context, one should also read Hughes's
"One More 'S' in the U.S.A." (1934), which reads like a radical song out
of the Wobblies' Little Red Song Book. The chorus reads:

Put one more s in the U.S.A.
To make it Soviet.
One more s in the U.S.A.
Oh, we'll live to see it yet.
When the land belongs to the farmers
And the factories to the working men—
The U.S.A. when we take control
Will be the U.S.S.A. then. (176–77)

One can easily imagine this poem sung at any number of the many Communist meetings and manifestations of the 1930s. (Unfortunately, this

poem would later be "sung" into the Senate Record by Senator Albert Hawkes as proof of Hughes's Communist sympathies.)

Interestingly, foregoing traditional African American expressive forms led Hughes to produce a poetry that was a little too "international," according to the standards in the proletarian movement for black writing. The Soviet critic Lydia Filatova took Hughes to task for not adhering to the formula for black writing when she wrote in *International Literature*, the organ of the Soviet-based International Union of Revolutionary Writers:

> Hughes's verses are impregnated with the spirit of proletarian interna-
> tionalism, which ought to be welcomed in every way. Yet the poet goes
> to extremes by *obliterating national boundaries* and to some extent *destroys the*
> *specific national atmosphere* of his poetry. *We are for an art that is national in form and*
> *socialist in content.* Hughes first of all is a poet of the Negro proletariat . . .
> The writer should present with the utmost sharpness the problems of his
> own race, but they must have a class aspect. The force of Hughe's [sic]
> poems will be stronger, the influence deeper, if he will draw closer to the
> Negro masses and *talk their language.* (107, emphases added)

Filatova criticizes Hughes for failing to incorporate the Black Nation Thesis into his poetry; his "un-African-American" poetry does not define African Americans in terms of black national characteristics, which, for Filatova, are largely marked by the possession of a black vernacular. Hughes seems to confound the CP's desire for an authentic black national expressive culture. In essence, Filatova criticizes Hughes for not being "black enough." Indeed, Hughes's poetry is not black "national in form" and is "socialist in content," which reflects his disagreement with the Comintern's Black Nation Thesis and its application by literary proletarians.

Aside from highlighting Hughes's internationalism, Filatova's criticism of Hughes's radical poetry is also important to note since it contradicts a number of contemporary studies that assume the CPUSA and the proletarian literary movement were responsible for Hughes's antinationalistic and unracialized writings from the 1930s. Referring in detail to Filatova's article but failing to mention her formula for "good" African American proletarian writing, Arnold Rampersad argues, for example, that the "communist aesthetic" is to blame for Hughes's loss of "essential identity" ("Langston Hughes and His Critics" 40). To the contrary, as William

Maxwell notes concerning Richard Wright's use of folk ideology, depression-era Communism granted black writers a "passport" to explore putatively authentic African American cultures (157). The misreadings of Hughes's radical poetry illustrate just how powerful ideologies of race, nation, and anticommunism continue to be within academia.

Nonetheless, Hughes's attempt to create a working-class aesthetic with mass appeal must be construed as a utopian project. It points to the problem of creating a truly collective poetry in form. That now quaint cityspeak of much 1930s poetry (the "hey buddy, can you spare a dime" line) cannot be construed as a universal American working-class dialect, a workers' "Esperanto" of sorts. Clearly such a dialect arose among second- and third-generation working-class European immigrant urban populations and became national primarily via mass media, such as film and radio in the 1930s. His erasure of national boundaries is therefore more profound than Filatova could imagine: the frequency of the national sound of his working-class Anglo-American poetry escapes her because it poses as universal. In truth, Hughes could not write a universal form for poetry, since language itself is "national in form," or, in other words, language is always cultural, and it is impossible to imagine what poetry would look and sound like in a communist world without race, nation, or class.

The noteworthy and rare exception to this rule about Hughes's radical poetry is "Sister Johnson Marches" (1937), the first sign of his return to dialect poetry and its radical possibilities. The poem contains a dialog between a working-class black woman and an unradicalized spectator at a May Day march. In response to the spectator's question, "Who are all of them people / Marching in a mass?," Sister Johnson replies, "Lawd! Don't you know? That's de working class!" (197). Like so much of his poetry that uses a black dialect, "Sister Johnson Marches" has the potential to speak powerfully to a multicultural working-class readership. Yet, even Hughes's mistaken attempt to transcend cultural diversity during the 1930s expresses a strength: it too is a testimony to Hughes's ardent desire not to be limited by the racialization/nationalization of black workers and writers, from either the Right or the Left.

In spite of its unnecessary formal limitations, Hughes's radical poetry is truly an accomplishment of modern poetry. It is unlike most other twentieth-century poetry, which, even when progressive, is often marred by spurious nationalisms. His radical poetry suggests that a multitude of cultural voices can, but does not necessarily, provide a rebuke to the Anglocentric and antiworking-class voices from whom we have heard too much. What is primary is what the voices are saying, since we can easily imagine, and perhaps know of, "minority" voices that espouse conservative ideologies inimical to the overcoming of racism, nationalism, and class exploitation. In short, Hughes's internationalist voice reminds us that a perspective that affirms constructed cultural or nationalist differences over fundamental, working-class interests is not necessarily oppositional to the political mainstream, and can have dire consequences for how we conceive of those old but persistent ideals for an egalitarian society.

6

Richard Wright's Critique
of Nationalist Desire

Not to plunge into the complex jungle of human relationships and analyze them is to leave the field to the fascists and I won't and can't do that.

Richard Wright

While serving as Director of the Harlem Bureau of the *Daily Worker* between 1937 and 1938, Richard Wright wrote an article for the newspaper praising the launching of *New Challenge*, a black American literary quarterly that published writers such as Ralph Ellison, Margaret Walker, and Langston Hughes. Wright was particularly excited about the quarterly because "[f]or the first time in Negro history problems such as nationalism in literature, perspective, the relation of the Negro to politics and social movements were formulated and discussed" ("Negro Writers Launch Literary Quarterly" 7). For those familiar with Wright's "A Blueprint for Negro Writing" (1937), first published in *New Challenge*, it is obvious that he was applauding his own planned contribution to the quarterly, as "Blueprint" deals first and foremost with the problem of nationalism for black writers. Moreover, since the *Daily Worker* article and the *New Challenge* essay were written in the middle of 1937, it is safe to say that Wright, then twenty-eight years old, was beginning to formulate just what sort of contribution to black American writing he hoped to make during the next few years. The literary works Wright composed between 1937 and 1941 focus explicitly on issues related to nationalism, although scholars have yet to explore this fact in depth.

Remarkably, his literary treatment of nationalism remains avant-garde since he reveals what many contemporary theorists have yet to disclose: a complex insight into the deep psychology of nationalism. While it is still unclear whether Wright had read works on psychoanalysis in the 1930s, his depictions of human psychology support many of the findings of psychoanalysis (especially those of Sigmund Freud and Melanie Klein) and, of course, of Marxism. From his own unique Marxist-psychoanalytic perspective, Wright portrays critically the insidious appeal of nationalistic ideas to the unconscious infantile desires of some working-class men. For Wright, since male workers are raised in a patriarchal society, their feelings of powerlessness can evoke feelings of emasculation, feelings that can be intensified for black men who are also oppressed by racism and are symbolically emasculated as "boys" in racist discourse. In somewhat Oedipal terms, Wright's black men are put in the position of having "to kill" the white man/father in order to cancel their "boy" status. Wright's concern is that black working-class men of the interwar period are apt to heed the call of black nationalists precisely because they promise a reclamation of manhood and the goal of disposing of the white father in the heroic quest for a black mother-land.

In *Lawd Today!* (completed in 1938 and posthumously published in 1963) and *Native Son* (1940), Wright represents particularly urban black men in the grips of such a racialized Oedipal struggle. His urban protagonists internalize the racist black boy/white father dichotomy and are thus psychologically caught between an impulse to act the "boy" who submits (in various ways) to whites and a desire to be the "man," which involves behaviors associated with the seemingly powerful white father. In other words, his protagonists seek to compensate for their socially conditioned feelings of impotence through fantasies of omnipotence, which are fed and formed by the "logic" of American racism, as well as the nationalistic and fascistic ideologies that flourished internationally in the 1930s. Both social-psychological and political factors contribute to a complex ethnic-nationalistic psychology for his protagonists, who unconsciously associate the attainment of manhood with the possession of a black "mother-land." However, while Wright represents the appeal of nationalism, he considers such an ideology incapable of self-reflexively addressing the very precondition for its being, that is, a racist class society. As the epigraph for this chapter suggests, Wright believed it vital to disclose and, therefore, to lessen the unconscious appeal of nationalism in order to make possible progressive political action for working-class men that is not determined by the self-defeating logics of American racism and nationalism. He believed that nationalism must be supplanted with a Communist ideology that could lead to the emancipation of the entire working class.

Before delving into Wright's Marxist-psychoanalysis of nationalism, we must first briefly work through his cultural history of black Americans, since only at the conclusion of a phase of that history do we find the black nationalist "resolution" of the Oedipal crisis alluded to above. It is well known that Wright was influenced by the Communist Party's (CP) understanding of nationalism, which was largely based on Stalin's popular book *Marxism and the National and Colonial Question* (1912). As Wright asserts in "A Blueprint for Negro Writing," he too believed that blacks had a common national culture originating in a "plantation-feudal economy" and subsisting in the Jim Crow political system of the South. The foundation of the modern black culture lies in the African American folk tradition of the blues, spirituals, work songs, and folk tales (99). Black social institutions, such as the black church, black sports, black business, black schools, and a black press, represent "a Negro way of life in America" (100).

However, for Wright, black cultural nationalism in the United States is neither as stable nor as progressive as the CP Black Nation Thesis makes out. On the contrary, such a shared way of life is the result of forced experiences of slavery and segregation that produced an *unwanted* black culture. Wright argues: "The Negro people did not ask for [their cultural nationalism], and deep down, though they express themselves through their institutions and adhere to this special way of life, they do not want it now. This special existence was forced upon them from without by lynch rope, bayonet and mob rule" (100). Such a nationalism is unstable for Wright because, even though he, like others in the CP, sees the social history of black Americans as a historical process, he also perceives "a complex movement of debased feudal folk toward a twentieth-century urbanization" that has occurred at a rapid pace (12 Million xix). The more or less homogenous black consciousness and cultural community resulting from provincial, southern material conditions were in the process of being eroded by modernization. Wright argues: "it is in industry that we encounter experiences that tend to break down the structure of our folk characters and project us toward the vortex of modern urban life . . . we are gripped and influenced by the world-wide forces that shape and mold the life of Western civilization" (12 Million 115). For Wright, the feudal black peasantry's liberation lay not in preserving or developing a black national culture in the South but in a historical overcoming of racialized identity and cultural nationalism. In other words, he only provisionally accepts the cultural nationalist identity of the postwar New Negro; he favors an urban, proletarian identity in the process of further socialization by modernity. In fact, nowhere in his literary work, nor in his more than two hundred articles written for the *Daily Worker*, do we find an endorsement for the CP's desire for a black republic in the southern Black Belt. Consequently, Wright was one to laud the historical movement toward modernity wherever he saw it. For example, one of his *Daily Worker* articles written in 1937 celebrates a former slave woman who became an active Communist in Harlem. "This woman," he writes, "has seen the face of her country changed more than once during her 71 years, and she has the strength, the courage, and the faith to fight and wait for still another change." He ends this short article by quoting her, saying for a second time, that "I live in the 20th Century" ("Born A Slave" 3), as if to underscore her own recognition that the movement from southern slave to urban Communist is part and parcel of the progressive movement of history itself. Like Langston Hughes, Wright was to the left of the CP on the "Negro Question."

While Wright identifies a cultural nationalism in decline, he nonetheless maintains that writers should acknowledge and strategically appropriate the varying degrees of cultural nationalism among black Americans. "Negro writers who seek to mold or influence the consciousness of the Negro people," asserts Wright, "must address their messages to them through the ideologies and attitudes fostered in this warping way of life" ("Blueprint" 101). It is important to note that "their messages" were (or should be) derived from "a Marxist conception of reality" (102). And, in this sense, Wright is consistent with the dominant thinking by Communist intellectuals of the time on "minority" literature. Hence, unlike Hughes, he is in accord with Soviet critic Lydia Filatova's position that minority literature should be "national in form and socialist in content" (107). In short, writers should represent the cultural nationalism of blacks from a socialist perspective by depicting national difference, inter-nationalist identity, and—echoing Georg Lukács's influential essay "Tendency or Partisanship" published in the *Partisan Review* in the 1930s—"society as something becoming rather than as something fixed and admired" ("Blueprint" 98–99). As *Uncle Tom's Children* (1940) attests, Wright was careful to represent contextually degrees of cultural nationalism in his characters, depicting virtually all of his southern characters in cultural nationalist terms. Big Boy from "Big Boy Leaves Home," Mann from "Down By the Riverside," Silas from "Long Black Song," and Aunt Sue from "Bright and Morning Star" are cultural nationalists by definition, although the events surrounding Johnny-Boy's political work and arrest move Aunt Sue leftward. The characters in *Uncle Tom's Children* whose cultural nationalism is weakest are precisely those who have been most influenced by modernity and the ideologies of modernity, such as Marxism. The communist-influenced Taylor from "Fire and Cloud" and (of course) Johnny-Boy from "Bright and Morning Star" are not purely cultural nationalists. Certainly Reverend Taylor and his followers are situated in a highly religious folk tradition, yet Taylor is able to unite and fight with white workers for economic relief. At one point Taylor exclaims, "Lawd knows, mabbe them Reds *is* right!" (157).

One therefore finds cultural nationalist identifications most eroded in his male urban protagonists from the 1930s, namely Jake Jackson from *Lawd Today!* and Bigger Thomas from *Native Son*. Jake and Bigger represent Wright's view of what happens when a first generation of "debased," male feudal folk are subjected to the modern ideologies and practices prevalent in northern urban centers (specifically Chicago): they become, as Wright explains of Bigger, "vague" cultural nationalists because, even though they are forced to identify as black, they do not identify with the black culture of their parents ("How Bigger Was Born" 527); Bigger, Wright tells us, "had become estranged from the religion and the folk culture of his race" (513). Bigger and Jake are "Negro nationalist[s] in a vague sense" only because of their "intense hatred of white people" (527), which serves (in place of a strong folk identity) to strengthen their identification as black.

Wright refunctions the wartime notion of a "No Man's Land" to designate the experience his urban male characters have of being in the interstice of two cultures, or, as Houston Baker argues, of having "black placelessness" (201). Only Wright's male urban protagonists are caught in the "No Man's Land," because they are "granted" by the patriarchal

economy more social intercourse with urban culture than his female characters. Most of the representations of Bigger and Jake (both who, significantly, grew up in the South) center on their being not at home but on
the streets or at work in "civilization," thus alienating them further from
their southern origins.

In contrast, while Wright really does not explore black female urban
subjectivity in any depth, the women he does create tend to be conservative or "traditional" believers in the system of religious values they inherited from the South or their southern mothers. In fact, black women,
and particularly black mothers, tend to be the repositories for cultural
nationalism in Wright's mind. He writes in 12 Million Black Voices that black
mothers are receptacles of "folk wisdom" (37) and that their consciousness "lies beyond the boundaries of the modern world" (135). As Baker
suggests, the black woman in Wright's vision uncritically "remains an
ahistorical remnant of folk culture" (213). Bigger's mother is an icon for
the cultural nationalist woman who is closely tied to the "old time" religion of Reverend Hammond. While Vera and Bessie from Native Son and
Lil from Lawd Today! are not as steeped in religion as Bigger's mother, they
are not represented as being in ideological crisis. Bessie, we read, is like
Bigger's mother, because (as far as Bigger is concerned), she passively
accepts her oppression (Native Son 278).

However, it should also be noted that Wright did not advocate such a
view of black women. Fortunately, modernity also revolutionized gender
identities and relations. Thus, in a Daily Worker article he wrote on Spanish
Harlem women who actively belonged to the La Pasionaria Branch of the
CPUSA, Wright appreciatively writes that "[t]hese women, descendants
and relatives of forebears who kept them firmly relegated to the home,
have leapt in the span of one short year from the kitchen into the arena
of international politics" ("Harlem Spanish Women Come Out of the
Kitchen" 5). Similarly, in an article entitled "Pullman Porters to Celebrate
12th Year of Their Union," Wright reports approvingly of the Brotherhood of Sleeping Car Porters' organization of thirty Women's Economic
Councils to provide support to the porters' labor struggles. Invoking
Lenin, he notes that "[f]reedom is the heritage of the strong and not until
the cook has come from her kitchen and learned to rule can the question
of the transformation of society become a reality" (3). Seen in light of
these articles, the social and political isolation of Bigger's mother pre-

vented her from recognizing the futility of religious submission before racist oppression. The radicalized Aunt Sue from Wright's "Bright and Morning Star" represents the antithesis of Bigger's mother.

Interestingly, black nationalism proper is only an issue for his male urban characters. Both Jake and Bigger have visions of a black state that they would like to rule. While undeveloped, their black nationalism equates freedom with national self-determination. Thus, the reflexive, weak cultural nationalism of most of his urban protagonists is supplemented by a black nationalism that imagines the creation of a black national state as a solution to U.S. racism. Ironically, black nationalism arises in the very place where cultural nationalist "folk" identities have been most dissolved by modern, urban conditions. This in part explains why the black nationalism Wright represents does not take root with his characters: urban culture and society have eroded the forced folk cultural identifications that nationalists attempt to exploit. The "double-consciousness" these characters possess prevents them from simply identifying as black "nationals" and from being chauvinist. Bigger, for example, so strongly identifies with "white" civilization that he cajoles Gus into "playing white" (18–20), one of their pastimes.

There are two important causes that explain why Jake and Bigger are attracted to black nationalist visions: 1) the psychological consequences of American racism, and 2) the predominance of postwar nationalisms in the 1930s.

In a number of his works, Wright suggests that black men have a particular psychic economy historically conditioned by a complex racist discourse and practice that, as we shall later see, lends itself to nationalists' appeals. He makes perfectly clear that the "Jim Crow education" of blacks in the South and the multiple, somewhat more subtle forms of racism in the North worked together in an attempt to arrest the psychological development of black American men. Black men/"boys" are infantilized by white society, making American racism conterminous with sexism, since the infantalization of black men symbolically aligns them with "women," that other figure long associated with weakness and dependency in patriarchal society. (Of course, the desire to project "weakness" onto black men truly betrays the white male working-class racist's own sense of social powerlessness under capitalism; the sense of powerlessness is disowned and often destroyed in an attempt to feel more strong—

gendered as "manly"—than one feels.) Within the racist, patriarchal logic of American racism, the "father"/"man" is none other than the white male who exercises authority over the movements of the supposedly helpless, dependent, and ignorant black "boy." The purpose of the psychological arrest is to stop autonomous actions that transgress "place" as defined by the racist structure and ideology of American society. Although indispensable to racist oppression, the legal arrest of black men signifies the failure of the ideology of racism.

Furthermore, Wright's texts suggest that the desire male children have to become men (usually like their fathers) is co-opted by white racist ideology in an important way: black males could become "men" by displacing and/or emulating the white father; the good "boy" obeys the white father's example and becomes like him. The internalization of the racist developmental logic constitutes the unconscious of his male characters and is characterized by a racialized Oedipal struggle against the white "father"/boss. In other words, the dynamics of psychological development are unconsciously mediated by racist ideology, and the super-ego itself contains the white "father's" judgment. In this way one can say that the "American" part of double-consciousness is expressive of the super (white) ego that views the black ego as despised and pitiable and yet represents cultural value, here coded as "white male." White folk, as Bigger says, live "[r]ight down here in my stomach" (22). As Abdul JanMohamed writes, "In order for subservience to be *automatic* it cannot be conscious; it has to become part of one's pre-conscious behavior pattern: precisely at the point where one's behavior is unconsciously controlled by a prevailing ideology, one has succumbed to a cultural hegemony" (117).

In many ways, Wright's depiction of the psychology of black working-class men also applies to white working-class men, since both are made to feel helpless under capitalism and can seek modes of escape that are infantile and nationalistic. For example, we can situate the masculinist iconography of a lot of proletarian art and literature within this framework: those images of hulky white workers underscore how powerless they may have felt during the Great Depression and thus function as wish fulfillments. However, it is essential to theorize the historicity of Wright's psychological understanding of urban black men—that is, how racism further belittles the black working class. The material conditions from which his male protagonists want to flee are those of racism and wage-labor in a capitalist society. Racist society is the painful, humiliating, and self-negating space that calls forth utopian spaces, including black nationalism. Such utopian spaces are shot through with the developmental conflicts of males as mediated by American racism and inter-war nationalism. In short, Wright's texts address the question of what happens when black working-class men who subjectively feel socially emasculated or socially disempowered are also assigned a "boy" status within the particular discursive formation of American racism.

The first point to be made here is that Wright's urban black protagonists have internalized the forced "boy" status and therefore seek ways to take control of their lives that are likewise mediated by a racist logic. That is, the options to act the "boy" or to become a "man"—certainly a major theme for many of Wright's stories—are not mutually exclusive. We find the twin impulses to be a "boy" and to be a "man" in the character of Jake from *Lawd Today!* Jake is unhappily married, reluctantly works as a postal clerk, and seeks gratification with a few coworkers during the off-hours. A typical Wright character, Jake is full of anger and cannot quite articulate the sources of or solutions to his feelings. Jake's basic problem is that circumstances are so set against him being black and working class that the novel is easily classified as naturalistic. Jake's infantile response to his oppression is most evident in his desire to leave the harsh realities of America and return to some imagined blissful, childlike state. He conceives of one of those blissful states as being in the possession of an idealized mother figure who takes care of him. In one passage, for example, he fantasizes about a woman with whom he feels like a "child nestling . . . into a mother's bosom" (36). In another passage he identifies with the "little boy blue" from a popular song who has helplessly lost but still desires a maternal woman who is "so beautiful," "so wonderful," and "so divine" (23). In short, he imagines a gratification that he lacks in the form of a regressive fantasy of being secure at the mother's breast. The breast is a symbol of a lost place of love, security, pleasure, and self-preservation for Jake. As Du Bois writes, only in "babyhood and in Europe" has the black man not experienced racism (*Souls* 37), potentially making the infantile fantasy all the more attractive.

Jake's desire to be taken care of is a sign of the larger problem he has of not taking responsibility for his *response* to the painful feelings (such as anger, jealousy, resentment, envy, and hatred) caused by his oppressive circumstances. His infantilism explains his attraction to the quick fix for his life, whether through the maternal fantasies, gambling, medical cure-alls, or alcohol abuse. One could say that he has modes of magical think-ing that are fed by the irrational culture that promises instant happiness, satisfaction, success, and so forth that Wright so thoroughly depicts.

Moreover, because Jake does not take responsibility for his feelings, thoughts, or actions, he tends to play the role of the helpless victim. He irresponsibly projects and disowns his own thoughts and actions that exacerbate an already bad situation. Aside from the absurdity of blaming Lil, his wife, for her tumor, he blames her for the entire condition of his life: "His eyes grew misty with tears, tears of hatred for Lil and tears of pity for himself. *My life is just all shot to hell. I wouldn't be in all this mess if it wasn't for her*" (20). Significantly, he verbally and physically abuses his wife because she depends upon him. In other words, he depreciates his wife—aptly named "Lil"—since she falls far short of his infantile desire for an idealized mother figure who gratifies his needs and removes the pains and frustrations he feels from his oppression. One can further argue that he attacks and threatens to kill her because he projects onto her and, ultimately, wants to destroy what he sees as his own weakness, his own sense of social and political helplessness, dependency, and, in a word, emasculation—all socially gendered as feminine. Thus, at the novel's end, after a series of defeats in and out of work, he returns home telling him-self, "*I'm going up and pay her off tonight! By Gawd, I'll teach her who's boss, who wears the pants*" (216). The sign of power for the emasculated Jake is the seemingly omnipotent boss who "wears [the] pants" that reveal by con-spicuously concealing the desired phallus. Jake has internalized his femi-nized "boy" status in a racist and patriarchal society, which explains why he despises both himself and Lil.

Wright's portrayal of Jake is dialectical, integrating the truth and falsity of Jake's position into a fuller analytical representation of his problem. Clearly, Jake is a victim of racism and class oppression, yet Wright also makes clear that his infantile behavior is nonetheless damaging to Lil and to himself. That is, Jake's response to his unjust circumstances (debt, discrimination, poverty) is one that Wright does not present as justified. The scene that brings the complexity of this issue to the fore is Jake's meeting with the postal Board of Review for his ill treatment of his wife.

The members of the board, two white men and one black man, are presented as sadistic individuals who take pleasure in their bureaucratic
power over Jake. Nevertheless, Jake's string of lies to save his job seems
absurdly defensive. He claims Lil, who complained to the board, lied
about being beaten. He pleads, "youall can't hold me responsible for a
crackbrained woman! She told youall them lies for pure evil black spite"
(124). He even goes so far as to say that, since he is proud to be black,
he "wouldn't do nothing on earth to drag down" his race (125)—even
though he demonstrates hatred for his "race" and his black body (by
subduing, for example, the "alien army" of kinks in his hair [23])
throughout the novel. Consequently, neither Jake nor the board are depicted as simply "good" or "right," which makes the truth of Howard's
(the black member of the board's) response to Jake's prevarication a hard
pill for Jake or the reader to swallow: "You should handle your affairs so
they won't come into this office. This isn't a nursery" (125). Ironically,
the post office is a kind of nursery as defined by the paternalistic, class
relations that position Jake as the helpless, bad boy in judgment by primarily white fathers/bosses (and one of their black lackeys or "Uncle
Toms") who hold a certain amount of power over him. They in large part
provoke and then punish Jake's babylike behavior.

Again, this is not to say that Jake himself has not opted out by his
continual flight from reality into the pleasure principle, a move, as Freud
tells us, always tied to the desire to forget one's own pain (*Beyond the
Pleasure Principle* 12–14). From this perspective, the mere fact of Jake's move
to Chicago can be viewed as a false flight not only from oppression (for,
as the text tells us, there is not much difference for the black man between
the North and South [180]), but also from the psychological pain resulting from the stronger social controls of black men in the South:

> When he went to the movies he always wanted to see Negroes, if there
> were any in the play, shown against the background of urban conditions,
> not rural ones. Anything which smacked of farms, chaingangs, lynchings,
> hunger, or the South in general was repugnant to him. These things had
> so hurt him once that he wanted to forget them forever; to see them again
> merely served to bring back the deep pain for which he knew no salve.
> (138)

Wright's Jake is far removed from (say) Sterling Brown's southern blacks
who, in spite hardships, find a nurturing folk culture of resistance. That

is, unlike Wright, Brown seems to have agreed with the dominant position of the Communist literary Left that black writers should embrace their national southern folk culture. Perhaps that is why Eugene Clay, a black Communist critic, published a sympathetic essay on *Southern Road* in *International Literature* only a year after Lydia Filatova published her criticism of Hughes for not creating poetry "national" in form. From Brown's view, Jake is one of those tragic figures with "sleek hair cajoled to Caucasian straightness" ("Children's Children" 108) who have lost their way in the North. As long as Jake tries to forget his emasculated "boy" status in a patriarchal and racist society, he is condemned to act the part. Indeed, throughout the day Jake continually wants to sleep, the sure way of forgetting by slipping into a state of unconsciousness.

Bigger is a more fully developed character than Jake and he therefore presents us with a refined psychological presentation of Wright's urban black male. Like Jake, Bigger is a character on the verge of losing control of his actions. He is about to "snap," and the only thing that keeps him from being torn asunder is his "dogged strength" (*Souls* 5), to use a phrase from Du Bois. The causes of his "tensity" are multiple, the most obvious being the abject racist conditions of his life on Chicago's South Side, which include the rat-infested room he must call his home and a lack of meaningful employment—in a word, a life of ghettoization. Wright's portrayal of Bigger's tension is itself remarkable for the times, since at the time of publication black workers had rarely been represented with such psychological depth and complexity.

What is more remarkable, however, is the way Wright portrays Bigger's response to the tension, and it is here that we find a psychological state similar to Jake's. Like Jake, Bigger simply wants to escape from his emotional tumult and so his methods are essentially regressive. He, too, seeks forms of escape that are infantile. The conclusive sign of this desire to regress is his masturbatory response to tension. Max, the mouthpiece of Wright's political understanding of Bigger, expresses the fundamental psychological truth of Bigger's character. As he tells the court in "defense" of Bigger's masturbating in a movie theater: "'Was not Bigger Thomas' relationship to his girl a masturbatory one? Was not his entire relationship to the whole world on the same plane?'" (468). The significance of these two lines should not be underestimated, for they succinctly encapsulate what Wright spends so much time disclosing in his novel.

Masturbation, as depicted here, is regressive because it allows for a narcissistic and sadistic way out of painful emotions. That is, instead of working to change the circumstances that give rise to these emotions, Bigger tries to discharge his emotions in ways that only create momentary relief for himself and pain or death for others. As Max suggests, Bigger sort of "masturbates" through Bessie, thus dehumanizing her by turning her into an object useful only for his satisfaction. Indeed, not much separates sex and murder for Bigger, since both "blot out" the other as a way to escape pain and/or to experience a narcissistic pleasure. "'All you care about is your own pleasure!'" exclaims his mother (7). Thus, when he has sex with Bessie before he kills her, we learn that she tells him not to force her to have sex but that the "loud demand of the tensity of his own body was a voice that drowned out hers" (270).

Masturbation here also signifies an idealized response to tension since he fantasizes that he has control of his life where he has virtually none. Of course, his reference to his penis as a "nightstick"—an emblem of police violence and power—in the masturbation scene is instructive (32), but perhaps more instructive is the fact that he also turns Bessie into an idealized mother figure who should exist only for him. Thus, once the "lessening of tension in his muscles" fades after murdering Mary (129), he decides to release the new quantity of tension that had accumulated while the racist Mrs. Dalton was questioning him. We read: "To go out now would be the answer to the feeling of strain that had come over him while talking to Mrs. Dalton. He would go and see Bessie. That's it!" (146). He immediately thinks of discharging his pain into Bessie and turns Bessie into an idealized womb he can occupy during sexual intercourse:

> He felt two soft palms holding his face tenderly and the thought and image of the whole blind world which had made him ashamed and afraid fell away as he felt her as a fallow field beneath him stretching out under a cloudy sky waiting for rain, and he slept in her body, rising and sinking with the ebb and flow of her blood, being willingly dragged into a warm night sea to rise renewed to the surface to face a world he hated and wanted to blot out of existence. (153)

The passage abounds with images of the maternal womb (fallow field, warm night sea). Like a fetus, he wants to be "inside" Bessie, "rising and sinking with the ebb and flow of her blood." As Joseph Skerrett writes, "Bessie is an oasis of motherly comfort in Bigger's world" (34). To be sure, he wants "a wholeness, a oneness" (*Native Son* 490) akin to what Freud refers to as "an oceanic feeling" one experienced as an infant in the womb or at the breast before the ego had learned to differentiate itself from the mother and to relate to people in other ways. Bigger can maintain this fantasy of Bessie only by depreciating and ultimately killing the Bessie that resists him and questions his confused thinking and harmful actions: "He wished he could clench his fist and swing his arm and blot out, kill, sweep away the Bessie on Bessie's face and leave the other helpless and yielding before him. He would then gather her up and put her in his chest, his stomach, some place deep inside him, always keeping her there even when he slept, ate, talked; keeping her there just to feel and know that she was his to have and hold whenever he wanted to" (159–60). Like Jake, he wants to cling only to his fantasy of an idealized mother who never frustrates him by always doing what he wishes, that is, by making the painful emotions of racism go away. From a Kleinian psychoanalytic perspective, this necessarily causes him to split Bessie in fantasy into a "good" mother and a "bad" mother (who withholds infantile gratification), and later to kill Bessie since she refuses to conform to his infantile fantasies.

Nevertheless, Jake and Bigger are struggling to be in control of their lives, which brings us to the issue of nationalism and, in particular, the second cause in Wright's black male protagonists' attraction to black nationalism, namely, the cultures of nationalism of the 1930s that he depicts in his novels. In essence, to quote Eric Hobsbawm, post-World War I nationalism "filled the void left by failure, impotence, and the apparent inabilities of other ideologies, political projects and programmes to realize men's hopes. It was the utopia of those who had lost the old utopias of the age of Enlightenment, the programme of those who had lost faith in other programmes" (*Nations and Nationalism* 144). Of course, we should add that nationalism was also the utopia for those who never were truly included in nor believed in "the old utopias" of the Enlightenment! In any case, Hobsbawm's linking of a sense of impotence, ideological confusion, and, in this context, the failure of bourgeois-democratic political ideals in America with an embrace of nationalism is compelling, since Wright's urban male protagonists are caught in a "No Man's Land" of disbelief, somewhere between their parents' southern "folk" beliefs and urban, mass-cultural ideologies. In particular, it is the patriarchal, nationalistic cultural density of Jake's and Bigger's Chicago that shapes the nationalist fantasies that function to compensate for their sense of emasculation. In fact, from the intrusive radio program commemorating Lincoln's birthday to newspaper headlines reporting Nazi nationalism and anti-Semitism, Lawd Today! is truly a study of cultures of nationalism in America circa 1935 and their effects on identity formation. Mass culture is less an explicit subject in Native Son but nonetheless an important one. Bigger, Wright tells us, "was trying to react to and answer the call of the dominant civilization whose glitter came to him through the newspapers, magazines, radios, movies, and the mere imposing sight and sound of daily American life" ("How Bigger" 513). The dominant "civilization" in the 1930s was becoming increasingly militaristic, fascistic, and nationalistic. Moreover, Hobsbawm adds, Hitler's ascension to power in 1933 greatly accelerated the trend of fascism, since "without Hitler's triumph in Germany, the idea of fascism as a universal movement . . . would not have developed," nor would it have had "serious impact outside of Europe" (The Age of Extremes 116–17). Bigger and Jake come of age during this fascisization of "civilization," and both characters are politically reactionary.

Within this context, Wright's male urban protagonists compensate for their sense of being a child, arrested, or in a "cesspool"—the original title of Lawd Today!—by identifying with patriarchal, nationalist figures. At several points in Lawd Today!, Jake has black nationalist fantasies. In one scene, Jake and his friends witness a Garveyite parade whose banner reads "ONWARD TO AFRICA" (105). Wright's depiction of the parade is highly satirical and reminiscent of those by A. Philip Randolph and Chandler Owen from the 1920s. The black nationalists come off as comical, deluded, and ironically influenced by the very white imperialists they theoretically reject. For instance, their leader is named the "Supreme Undisputed Exalted Commander of the Allied Imperial African War Councils unto the Fourth and Last Generations" (106). Nonetheless, on hearing the leader's title, Jake exclaims in awe, "'Jeeesus!'" Interestingly, after criticizing them on their program to go back to Africa, Jake and his friends "agree with the music" of the parade, which recalled "memories of those Sunday mornings in the South when they had attended church"

(110). Immediately following this protonational identification, Jake, "out of the depths of a confused mood," says "'You know . . . maybe them folks is right, who knows?'" (110). The parade continues to work on Jake's mind and finally develops into an elaborate fantasy immediately following being harassed by the white patriarchal postal inspector. Here we read:

> If only there was something he could do to pay the white folks back for all they had ever done! . . . He felt the loneliness of his black skin. Yeah, *some foreign country ought to whip this Gawddamn country! Some black country ought to do it!* He remembered the parade . . . *Yeah, maybe they's right. Who knows?* He saw millions of black soldiers marching in black armies; he saw a black battleship flying a black flag; he himself was standing on the deck of that black battleship surrounded by black generals; he heard a voice commanding: "FIRE!" *Boooooom!* A black shell screamed through black smoke and he saw the white head of the Statue of Liberty topple, explode, and tumble into the Atlantic Ocean . . . *Gawddamn right!* (143–44)

He continues to build "dreams of a black empire" and imagines an "epic where black troops were about to conquer the whole world" (144). Jake's imperialistic fantasy is clearly informed by news of Hitler's war against Jewish people and the start of his European conquest. The "Exalted Commander" is cast as a Hitler who will supposedly unify people. Later in the text the nameless black voices that compose part 2, chapter 4 confirm the importance of German and Italian nationalism to Wright's characters' thinking when we read, "'it'd take a strong guy to make all these [multi-ethnic American] folks come under one command.' 'You telling me?' 'Like old Hitler . . .' '. . . and Mussellinni'" (183–84). The key point here is that the urban mass culture dominated by the ideologies of postwar nationalism transforms Jake's "vague" cultural nationalism—forced blackness and hatred of whites—into black nationalism proper. In the above scenes, the various interwar nationalisms—American nationalism, German nationalism, Italian nationalism, and black nationalism—bombard Jake and his friends, and, in their minds, all nationalisms are the same, since all nationalists appeal to their desires for power and control over their lives. On reading the Garveyites' Preamble that speaks of "One God! One Aim! One Destiny!" one of the characters says, "Boy, that sounds like the Constitootion!" (109). From his xenophobia, to his Republicanism, to the military metaphors he uses to describe the subduing of his hair, Jake proves himself to be a fine product of the nationalistic fascisization of the world.

In *Native Son* as well there are numerous passages that exemplify Wright's understanding of the psychological and cultural underpinnings of black nationalism. As suggested above, Bigger is a man who rejects his mother's black folk culture and is dazzled by American popular culture (*Native Son* 278) and, like Jake, identifies with the rabid nationalist projects of the 1930s. We read: "Dimly, he felt that there should be one direction in which he and all other black people could go whole-heartedly . . . He liked to hear of how Japan was conquering China; of how Hitler was running the Jew to the ground; of how Mussolini was invading Spain . . . He felt that some day there would be a black man who would whip the black people into a tight band and together they would act and end fear and shame" (130). Bigger identifies with these supposedly nationalist leaders because they are father figures or führers who "whip" the imagined helpless black masses into shape for their own good. Both Jake and Bigger identify with nationalists precisely because they are authoritarian, supposedly omnipotent, and historically have been patriarchal to the core.

An irony resides here, because his male urban protagonists' displacement from the South (and its white father-black boy dichotomy that narrowly defines place) results in the reemergence of the super-white ego in black face. That is, displacement to a contradictory urban environment that promises all but grants little—and the desires, anxieties, and tensions that accompany it—has produced a counterdesire for placement structurally akin to that from which they originally fled. The discourse of American racism has worked so effectively that the original desired usurpation of the (southern) master and desire for freedom has produced (within the racist wage-slavery of the urban society) a desire for a black master, motivated by his characters' infantile "reflex urge towards ecstasy, complete submission, and trust" ("How Bigger" 528). Wright's texts suggest that the frustrations of the No Man's Land and the appeal of nationalism are both symptomatic of the failure of American capitalism to provide political, economic, and psychological stability conducive to his characters' desires for happiness.

The black master, then, functions as the father figure for these socially emasculated men without fathers. (In *Lawd Today!* there is no mention of

Jake's parents, and in *Native Son* we learn that Bigger's father was killed in a riot in the South [85], the ultimate act of social emasculation for a black man and Jim Crow lesson for a black son.) Bigger, in particular, is represented as a man in search of a father figure; hence, the black führer is a suitable compensatory image and the various depression-era fascisms "simply appealed to him as possible avenues of escape" (130). He identifies with Hitler and Mussolini because he desires the control and power that have been culturally gendered as masculine. As he tells Max: "a guy gets tired of being told what he can do and can't do. You get a little job here and a little job there . . . You don't know when you going to get fired . . . *You just keep moving all the time*, doing what other folks say. *You ain't a man no more*" (408, emphasis added). To be a "man" is finally to be free from the displacement—the "moving all the time." The fascist father figure is the one who defines place for all. Likewise, Wright suggests that the fascist dream of omnipotence appeals to the desire to control what Wright calls "a hot and whirling vortex of undisciplined and unchannelized impulses" produced by modernity ("How Bigger" 520). The fascistic, nationalistic projects of Jake and Bigger are another way they imagine a freedom from their emotional tumult. And it is important to note that, in truth, their fantasies of a black master are mediated by a desire to be "white," which they equate with being a desired and powerful object. In essence, as the Garveyite parade and Bigger and Gus's game of mimicry suggest, to be a political leader is to "play white." The "dual narcissism" of which Frantz Fanon writes about in *Black Skin, White Masks*—that white is right and black is beautiful—merge here: by indulging their fantasies, the two characters display their ego-ideal of the white man who *looks* black or the black man who *acts* white. Conflated are the concepts of white-father-nationalist-fascist-man as opposed, in, the final analysis, to the concept of "black boy."

The black nation (ruled by the black father) thus functions as a wishful political and psychic economy: the white father is dethroned, the black "boy" becomes the (white) "father," creating a (home) place that, because the white father is usurped, "end[s] fear and shame" (*Native Son* 131). The psychological goal of nationhood in these novels is a type of unity that, based on the male fantasies, is infantile, since the object is to reclaim "a wholeness, a oneness" (*Native Son* 490) associated with an idealized infantile state that views the nation as a womb mother or an originary site of pleasure. The internal torment and desires these characters display generated in large part by the super (white) ego is projected out and solved in fantasy as if it were solely an external problem.

A dialogue immediately following the passage from Lawd Today! on the necessity of a Hitler or Mussolini for national unification cited earlier establishes the link between nationalism, maternity, and masculinity in the unconscious of the text:

> "Well, I reckon the best thing for a guy to do is get together with a woman."
> "State Street Mama!"
> My name is Jim Taylor
> My John is a whaler
> And my balls weigh ninetynine pounds
> If you know any ladies
> Who want to have babies
> Just tell 'em Jim Taylor's in town . . ."
> "Hahaha!"
> "Hohoho!" (184)

The maternal woman or the imagined black state (whose shorthand here reads: black "State [Street] Mama" land) provides an escape from the pain caused by racism to a place without the "fear and shame" of the internalized white father's gaze and a reclaimed (and exaggerated) sense of masculine potency ("balls"). In the imagination of these characters, the mama-land lies the greatest distance from no-man's land. The patriarchal core of the nationalist fantasy is also exposed here, since these characters have recourse to sexist ideas precisely when the nationalist fantasy fails them. And, as with the threatened child in the Oedipal situation who clings desperately to the mother, his urban male protagonists demonstrate a tyrannical possessiveness over the imaginary black mother-land and/or its imperfect human substitutes. Aside from Bigger and Jake's attempts to control Bessie and Lil, respectively, Lawd Today! portrays male possessiveness over the motherland substitutes in the scenes where Jake and his friends are stimulated by looking at pornography depicting a woman subjected to a man who "rid[es] her like a stallion" (186) as well as when Jake tells his friends: "'I'd like to horsewhip every black cunt who so much as looks at a white man'" (140). Thus, the desire for the black motherland is simultaneously expressive of both the desire to regress *and* a desire to advance to the position of the father (who appears to possess the mother). The black nation is the Oedipal fantasy writ large in political terms, where the infantile desires for a womb/breast-like "oneness" and paternity are simultaneously met.

Clearly, Wright does not advocate such a political and psychic economy. His representation of a highly patriarchal black nationalism as *just one more* illusion of freedom for his characters should make us pause at the unfair criticisms of his work that mistakenly conflate the sexism of Jake and Bigger with Wright's own stance. On the contrary, it is one of Wright's major achievements to write insightfully about the social and psychological disorders that can afflict (black) working-class men. In this way, he was able to explore why the impossible, "childish" politics of the black nationalists ("How Bigger" 520; *Black Boy* 337) appeal to otherwise grown men. Indeed, Wright's depression-era work shows that there is no going back to a folk way of life. More important, there is no going forward to a black nation-state for these twentieth-century black men: in spite of sociopsychological neurotic desires created by American racism, black male identities are too complex for any kind of exclusive "black" identity/nation.

The question we are left with is why the novels do not represent Wright's alternative to the neurotic and reactionary protagonists, namely, black communists. (The undeveloped and minor character of the Communist Duke in *Lawd Today!* only functions as another occasion for the reader to witness Jake's conservatism.) Instead of assuming some grand anti-Communist narrative that informs his urban fiction years before his actual break with the CP, I think it is more instructive to see how Wright's urban fiction (particularly *Native Son*) represents the working through of infantile desires and black nationalist fantasies rather than an exemplary image of a black communist. In this sense Max can be read as a figure for the analyst who provides the opportunity for Bigger to talk and to think his way through the feelings that he had previously and murderously discharged. Due to Max, Bigger comes a long way, for he finally is able to see others as human beings, that is, he projects less by the novel's end. Certainly, by perceiving Max as a father figure (which Max encourages by constantly referring to Bigger as "son") Bigger's transference continues through to the last page. But even here Max as father figure suggests Bigger's psychological and political development: unlike the punishing father/führer figure who contributes to his omnipotent fantasies, the nurturing Max teaches Bigger how to think about his feelings and actions, and, more important, he teaches the hard lesson of the reality principle concerning the slow process of collective social change. The premature termination of the "therapy" for Bigger—the death sentence—does not affect the cultural work of the novel, since, in the last analysis, what is at stake is that the reader continues thinking through his own potentially destructive emotions and ideas—presuming that Bigger's psyche is not all that unique, as Wright claims in "How Bigger Was Born." Or for a reader without such psychological issues, the end of the novel would prompt further reflection on how an unresolved social and/or racialized Oedipal struggle for men contributes to sexism and makes working-class men susceptible to the call of nationalism. In either case, the reader comes away with a better sense of the interrelatedness of the oppressive social system and neurosis. Dialectically, then, in Wright's urban fiction, the path to socialism involves retracing and understanding the hazardous, regressive missteps people may take in hope to be free from the pain of social inequality. The novel ends where revolutionary action may begin.

The central place where Wright reserves his depictions of desirable alternatives to Jake and Bigger are the articles he published in the *Daily Worker* between 1937 and 1938. One could cite the many articles he wrote on progressive black leaders, such as James Ford, A. Philip Randolph, and Louise Thompson; the unknown black working-class people who fought for better lives in their neighborhoods and communities (many of whom Wright reports were women!); or those who fought for democracy in Spain against the fascists. The very titles of the articles—"American Negroes in Key Posts of Spain's Loyalist Forces," "Walter Garland Tells What Spain's Fight Against Fascism Means to the Negro People," "James W. Ford Celebrates 44th Birthday—Leads Progressives in Harlem Community," and "Negro Social Worker Hails Housing, Education in Spain"—express Wright's admiration for the black working-class and Communist leaders.

In a *Daily Worker* article entitled "Mrs. Holmes and Daughters [sic] Drink From the Fountain of Communism" (1937), Wright sympathetically reports, for example, on an impoverished black working-class woman from Harlem who explains to her daughter why she joined the CPUSA. Like other workers during the depression, the unemployed Mrs. Holmes accepted an invitation by a Communist neighbor to go to the Workers'

Alliance for food and comradeship. At the Workers Alliance, Wright explains, Mrs. Holmes also learns "how to stand up and fight" (5). Soon afterwards she accepted an invitation to join the CP "to help them to help others as they had helped me" (5). On hearing her mother's story, the daughter, who had been studying nursing at a Catholic convent in the South, decides to join the CP as well. Wright ends his article by stating:

> Paradoxically, the hard clenched fist is not the only symbol of Communism. There is a fist thrust into the faces of capitalist exploitation, but there also is a hand of compassion stretched forth to the poor and downtrodden.
>
> The clenched fist is not a bluff. It's a fist reaching for power. And the hand of compassion is not sticky with false kindness. It is not the kind that gives Hearst Milk Funds; instead it touches the downtrodden to quicken them to new life, to give them courage to struggle for the possession of the earth on which they live. (5)

Wright's respect for this working-class mother and her daughter is also borne out in the dialogic style of his article; he lets them speak, and only afterwards does he present his own perspective that includes his class hatred for the exploitative bourgeoisie and sympathy for the exploited working class.

These articles compose part of a larger panorama of black leaders to be emulated in various ways (including Frederick Douglass, Nat Turner, and Angelo Herndon) written about by contributors to the Daily Worker. Lawd Today! and Native Son need to be (re)placed next to these articles, for in them we find men and women who have subjectively overcome racism enough to struggle objectively for an end to inequality. Wright reports about black workers and leaders who have overcome the racist "Manichean concept of the world" (Fanon, Black Skin 44–45) and no longer conceptualize liberation in terms of color: present struggles and the desired future society of socialism are not driven by the desires to be white or black, slave or boss, boy or father. For Wright, the Communists' ideal of socialism—a social order without sexism, classes, and racism—as well as the very struggle for the ideal—provides a channel for, and ultimate solution to, the kinds of emotions and desires of Jake and Bigger. He reports of black men and women who, in conjunction with white workers and Communists, *actively work to change themselves by changing their circum-*

stances. As many events of the 1930s suggest, through multiracial praxis workers were able substantially to defeat the debilitating racist preconceptions that function to keep people separate and unequal.

Native Son illustrates this point somewhat, since both Bigger and Jan are forced to give up their faulty perceptions of each other only by struggling together. To recall, after having met with Jan and directly after one of his "sessions" with Max, Bigger reflects that "[i]f that white looming mountain of hate were not a mountain at all, but people, people like himself, and like Jan—then he was faced with a high hope the like of which he had never thought could be" (418). The hypothesis about the "white looming mountain" seems borne out, since Bigger's last request in the novel divests Jan of his putative "master" status: "Tell Mister . . . Tell Jan hello" (502). Bigger has learned to work through his fantasy only by confronting reality, or, rather, by having reality confront him when flight is no longer an option.

In the end it is a young black man named Edward Strong that Wright had in mind when he fictionalized black Communists in his powerful collection of short stories, *Uncle Tom's Children*. Strong, whom Wright interviewed for one of his *Daily Worker* articles, was the executive secretary of the Communist-led Southern Negro Youth Congress, which fought for jobs for black youth, civil rights, and against war and fascism ("Negro Youth On March 3"). Both a cause and an effect of a new progressive and militant subjectivity in the southern heartland of racism during the Great Depression, Strong beat one of the greatest odds in America: he fought actively with black and white workers against racist oppression. We know that Wright was so impressed with Strong that he not only wrote an article on him but also used his words for his epigraph to *Uncle Tom's Children*. "Uncle Tom is dead," declares Strong, precisely because black men and women have taken "their destiny into their own hands" and, more important, "are breaking down the wall between the two races" (3). In other words, for Wright, the dialectical overcoming of racism and nationalism (and their complex psychological consequences) occurs through repeated multiracial action against the social system founded on racism and slavery. Bigger and especially Jake represent the tragic consequences of the racist and nationalistic ideologies that function to prevent the class consciousness and solidarity needed to create a better world for the entire working class.

Afterword

Beyond Twentieth-Century Nationalisms in the Study of African American Culture

Let us new lessons learn,
All workers,
New life-ways make,
One union form:
Until the future burns out
Every past mistake.

Langston Hughes, "Open Letter to the South"

In spite of the powerful critiques of nationalism by black socialists and the black literary Left, not to mention the enormous body of socialist political and literary theory available for study, most scholars of black literature and culture remain entrenched in anticommunist and pronationalist theoretical paradigms. One indicator of the predominance of this nationalist perspective is the tendency of editors of African American literature anthologies to exclude from consideration radical black texts that fall outside of its parameters, thus leaving us with a skewed sense of black literary and political history. A good example of political/literary exclusion can be found in the Norton *Anthology of African American Literature* (1997). The editors, Nellie McKay and Henry Louis Gates, have admirably compiled and introduced most of the material. However, not once in their introductions do they refer to the importance of the Bolshevik Revolution to black American writers. They only refer in passing to the socialist *Messenger* in their introduction to the Harlem Renaissance but claim that socialism had no impact on black writers. Not surprisingly, they include two speeches by Marcus Garvey but none by Garvey's socialist critics. Nor do they mention the influence of the CPUSA or Communist magazines and organizations on black writers in the 1930s. And their headnote for Langston Hughes fails to reference the large quantity of revolutionary literature he wrote during the Great Depression. Instead, the editors muse that "in the 1930s Hughes's main concern was *probably* the theatre" (1253, emphasis added). Hence, they exclude Hughes's and Richard Wright's overtly internationalist poetry and fiction, and even go so far as to add sections from *Black Boy* that tell of Wright's final disagreements with the CPUSA. The editors also stretch the dates of the Harlem Renaissance to 1940, thereby canceling out the issues and events of the "Red Decade" for black writers. We find similar misrepresentations of black literary history and black writers replicated in *The Prentice Hall Anthology of African American Literature* (2000) and *Call and Response: The Riverside Anthology of the African American Literary Tradition* (1998), the latter dismissing the literary and political value of Hughes's Communist verse with a trite, "Most of these verses lack an original voice" (Hill 1013). The editor's criterion of originality for African American literature barely conceals here the cultural nationalist criteria of a black vernacular and subject matter. As Bill Mullen critically notes, one of *Call and Response's* major organizing devices is "the 'nation within a nation' theme outlined in the Introduction" ("Breaking the Signifying Chain" 150). Like many scholars of black culture, the editors of these anthologies seem comfortable with the idea that black culture in the United States is and should be either African or American, either globally racial or locally national.

Certainly, there are important historical explanations for the resistance of these scholars to radical African American literature and theory. While the clamor of the Cold War period may have passed, its ubiquitous effects continue to limit critical thinking about black culture. It appears that the old "spectre of communism" has given rise in this so-called postcommunist world to a spectre of anticommunism that also imagines capitalism is the best of all possible worlds (with a little reform, perhaps). Destroying the theoretical gains (not to mention many of the practical victories) of the remarkable class-conscious interlude of the Great Depression, anticommunism has nearly abolished class as an analytic concept for cultural study. Not only have the unabashedly bourgeois states and cultures contributed to the current phase of anticommunism but so has the anti-Marxist revisionism of the old socialist movements. This revisionism, which I earlier analyzed in relation to the Popular Front period, led to a betrayal of the working classes, "black, white, olive, yellow, brown," as Hughes puts it in "The Same," and to the restoration of capitalism in China and Russia. Both its bourgeois detractors and many of its "socialist" supporters have so distorted the philosophy and political goals of communism that it is not surprising to encounter its marginalization in/omission from literary anthologies of all kinds. One important exception, as I mentioned in chapter 5, is the *Heath Anthology of American Literature*, which recognizes the centrality of radical literature to the American literary tradition. Unfortunately, without a comprehensive understanding of the tradition of Marxism, as well as a left critique of Russia and China, one can easily assume that Marxism, as a theory for understanding and changing culture and society, is truly "dead."

The difficulties, mistakes, failures, and defeats of the last century are everyone's legacy, a legacy that one must struggle with, especially if one has progressive scholarly and political concerns. To be sure, since there is no "outside" to modern history, even the nationalist basis of so much current scholarship is motivated by the same antiracist and democratic politics that motivated the interwar writers. In the absence of a sizable non-nationalist left-wing presence in the United States, the spate of recent publications of African American literary anthologies more specifically reflects the increasing ethnic specialization of literature that aims to correct the omissions and misrepresentations of earlier Eurocentric fields of study. Thus, inherently contradictory, African American specialization usefully legitimates the study of black culture as a crucial component of higher education while it simultaneously reinforces the perception that the diverse literary, vernacular, and political cultures of black Americans are unconnected or only tangentially related to the multileveled diversity of class society. Given the dominant institutional and social frameworks that trumpet the values of multiculturalism as a natural outgrowth of the dual (or "hyphenated") bourgeois nationalisms that are said to make America great, it makes sense, although problematically, that the concept of "difference" prevails in cultural studies.

This current historical and theoretical impasse, abounding in contradictions, presents serious challenges to black cultural studies. As I have intimated throughout this study, in order to begin to overcome this impasse it will be imperative to return to and carry forward the strongest ideas of the black socialists as well as their counterparts of all "colors." The historical materialist basis of the literary and political Left's critique of ideology provides some of the tools to move beyond the false solutions of bourgeois and "revolutionary" nationalism, both of which end up in the very theoretical quandaries and political failures that the international working class pays for in superexploitation, oppression, and war.

One of the key materialist perspectives that we need to recuperate is the radical historicization of racial/national identity. Only by historicizing subjectivity can we demonstrate how our racialized/nationalized selves are politically *forced*, as Richard Wright argues, and not simply the result of an individual decision bearing little or no relationship to the dominant discourses and institutions of power. We need not look far for examples of the continuing relevance of the black socialists' materialist critique of identity. In the political aftermath of the attacks on the World Trade Center and the Pentagon on September 11, 2001, to cite a particularly tragic example, many people in the United States began to feel more American than they had felt in years. The *patriotic* feelings did not simply emerge from viewing the destruction of human lives, however. After all, one can empathize with people even if they are not "American." Rather, people's feelings were manipulated by the flag waving of the U.S. government, corporations, and the mass media, as well as the countless flag vendors on street corners throughout the United States. The manufactured patriotism of the moment called forth and strengthened people's prior training to identify with America (whether in grade school, or as a subject constructed by the popular culture, or through the international allure of the wealth and power of U.S. imperialism). The mass culture worked overtime to ensure that the pity people felt, to invoke Aristotle, was only the result of witnessing the unmerited misfortune of people like themselves, "Americans." At the same time, the media-generated and government-sponsored anti-Arab racism (in the detention of more than one thousand people of Middle Eastern descent and the enactment of the "Patriot Act," for instance) intensified the racialization of the U.S. population. "Racial profiling," a term that smacks of the pseudoscientific racist discourses of yesteryear, functioned to "profile" not only Arabs (as it has blacks and Latinos) but all people in the United States who were encouraged to view their own already racialized identities relationally. In short, as an analysis of recent events indicate, one is not born "black," "white," "brown," or "American," but only becomes so within the triumphant discourses and social institutions that maintain that one's skin pigmentation, surname, place of birth, or residence are somehow definitive of identity and loyalties. The world system that nurtured the writers of the Harlem Renaissance and the proletarian literary movement is not so different from ours as to invalidate the socialists' critiques of nationalist identity.

Yet, the historicization of identity, which, after all, is a defining feature of most cultural studies, cannot in itself lead beyond the impasse. What defines more precisely the historical materialist critique from other antiessentialist theories is its class analysis of ideology. Here as well the work of the interwar black Left merits serious reconsideration, since in their best work they employ class analyses that cut through the multiple mystifications that pass for liberatory ideas while in truth further subjugating the multicolored working class. For them, nationalism and racism were not just discourses of ill-defined power, much less of "white" power, but, rather, ideologies that serve the interests of the bourgeoisie. When the black Marxists viewed oppression internationally, they perceived that the ideologies of race or nation could not explain why white bosses treated their white workers in the United States so horribly or why a civil war between peoples of the same "nation" and "race" occurred in Spain. And since, as they believed, class interests underlay (even if in distorted form) the innumerable conflicts of their time—from those on the shop floor of the factory, to the mail room of the postal service, and the racist courtrooms in Scottsboro, Alabama—they committed themselves to producing a class-conscious literature and criticism that could help to educate workers of all colors about their own class interests. In a word, Marxian class analysis provided them with the means to sort out what ideas can in practice help to realize their core desires for an egalitarian world. In the midst of their struggles against the dominant ideologies they made mistakes, of course. Nonetheless, their errors mostly resulted from losing sight of the class structure of their society and the need to consider all political and cultural questions in relation to the crucial issue of advancing the struggle to emancipate the entire working class from the regime of capital. In relation to our present moment, such a perspective helps to safeguard against the ongoing nationalist and racist justifications for imperialist war abroad and political repression at home, as well as the well-intentioned but unworkable critiques of cultural particularism that find refuge in universalisms.*

In brief, the kind of internationalist framework I am suggesting for

---

* Noteworthy as a contemporary universalist critique of race and nation is Paul Gilroy's recent book, *Against Race*. Gilroy boldly challenges racist and fascist ideologies of identity and proposes an alternative perspective he terms "planetary humanism," a concept to overcome the color line based on humanity's universal biology and experiences.

black studies, modeled on the best radical writings and practice of the last century, philosophically represents a broadening out of concerns, a widening of social and cultural contexts, and a stronger commitment to linking our work on African American culture to the larger goal of forwarding the liberatory struggles of all oppressed working-class peoples. After at least a hundred years of important cultural work that has located, explained, and validated cultural differences—historically necessary work to help refute Eurocentrism—the time has come to establish equally the nature of shared, working-class cultures, identities, and interests. An internationalist reconceptualization of black culture would have a liberating impact on everything we do, from the organizing of conferences, the editing of literary anthologies, and the practicing of criticism, to teaching. At a minimum, it would encourage healthy debates about the desire to organize our work according to the too fashionable principle of racial, national, and cultural difference that divides academic workers into a kaleidoscope of pseudospecializations.

While one cannot predict the future, it is safe to say that as the capitalist world system experiences ever more crises of overproduction (or "recession" as we now say), more interimperialist rivalry (or "globalization"), and war ("humanitarian intervention"), we can expect ideologies of race and nation to continue to play an important role in misleading the working class to attack each other instead of the systemic causes of their oppression. Black cultural studies will make a progressive difference in the forthcoming struggles if, as Langston Hughes wrote during another time of crisis, it can "smash the old dead dogmas of the past— / To kill the lies of color / That keep the rich enthroned / And drive us to the timeclock and the plow / Helpless, stupid, scattered, and alone—as now" ("Open Letter" 160).

"The recurrence of pain, disease, humiliation and loss of dignity, grief, and care for those one loves," writes Gilroy, "can all contribute to an abstract sense of a human similarity powerful enough to make solidarity based on cultural particularity appear suddenly trivial" (17). Without an analysis of the *structural inequalities* of capitalism, however, Gilroy's "planetary humanism" becomes another ideological variant of universal philosophies (such as nationalism) that claims for itself the power to bridge the class divide endemic to capitalism. Additionally, the pain Gilroy views as a basis for his humanism belongs disproportional to the world's working classes; only in that sense, when analyzed as stemming from specific material conditions (such as exploitation, war, lack of adequate health care, etc.), can pain indeed become a basis for working-class solidarity that would make "cultural particularity appear suddenly trivial."

Bibliography

African Blood Brotherhood. "Garvey Shows His Hand." *Crusader* 5.2 (Oct. 1921): 23–24.

———. "Program of the A.B.B." *Crusader* 5.2 (Oct. 1921): 15–18.

———. "A Race Catechism." *Crusader* 1.1 (Sept. 1918): 11.

Allen, James S. *The Negro Question in the United States.* New York: International Publishers, 1936.

Anderson, Benedict. *Imagined Communities: Reflections on the Origin and Spread of Nationalism.* New York: Verso, 1983.

Baker, Houston, "On Knowing Our Place." *Richard Wright: Critical Perspectives Past and Present.* New York: Amistad Press, 1993. 200–25.

Balibar, Etienne. "The Nation Form: History and Ideology." *Race, Nation, Class: Ambiguous Identities.* London: Verso, 1991. 86–106.

Barnes, Albert C. "Negro Art and America." *The New Negro.* 1925. Ed. Alain Locke. Introd. Arnold Rampersad. New York: Atheneum, 1992. 19–25.

Berry, Faith. *Langston Hughes: Before and Beyond Harlem.* Westport, Conn.: Lawrence Hill, 1983.

Bixler, J. S. "Spirituals to Swing: 2." *New Masses* 26 Dec. 1939: 28.

Bloch, Ernst. *The Principe of Hope.* Vol. 1. Trans. Neville Plaice et al. Cambridge, Mass.: MIT, 1995.

Braithwaite, William Stanley. "The Negro in American Literature." *The New Negro.* 1925. Ed. Alain Locke. Introd. Arnold Rampersad. New York: Atheneum, 1992. 29–44.

Brennan, Timothy. "The National Longing for Form." *Nation and Narration.* Ed. Homi K. Bhabha. New York: Routledge, 1990. 44–70.

Briggs, Cyril. "The Decline of the Garvey Movement." 1931. *American Communism and Black Americans: A Documentary History, 1930–1934.* Ed. Philip S. Foner and Herbert Shapiro. Philadelphia: Temple University Press, 1991. 78–83.

———. "The Old Negro Goes: Let Him Go in Peace." *Crusader* 2.2 (Oct. 1919): 9–10.

———. "Two Negro Papers Discover Americanism." *Crusader* 4.5 (July 1921): 10.

Browder, Earl. "For National Liberation of the Negroes! War Against

White Chauvinism!" *The Communist Position on the Negro Question.* n.p. c. 1933. 3–18.

——. *The People's Front.* New York: International Publishers, 1938.

——. "Who Are the Americans?" *What Is Communism?* New York: Workers Library, 1936. 17–23.

Brown, Sterling. "Children's Children." *Southern Road.* Introd. Sterling Stuckey. Boston: Beacon, 1974. 107–8.

——. *Southern Road.* Introd. Sterling Stuckey. Boston: Beacon, 1974.

Burrell, Theo. "African Blood." *Crusader* 5.3 (Nov. 1921): 6, 32.

Clay, Eugene. "The Negro in Recent American Literature." *American Writers' Conference.* Ed. Henry Hart. New York: International Publishers, 1935. 145–53.

——. "Sterling Brown: American Peoples' Poet." *International Literature* 2.8 (June 1934): 117–22.

Colson, William N. "The New Negro Patriotism." 1919. *Voices of a Black Nation: Political Journalism in the Harlem Renaissance.* Ed. Theodore G. Vincent. Trenton, N.J.: Africa World Press, 1973. 67–69.

Communist International. "The Conspiracy of Munich." *The Communist International* 15.10 (Oct. 1938): 875–85.

——. "Program of the Communist International: Together With the Statutes of the Communist International." New York: Workers Library, 1929.

——. "Resolution of the Communist International, 1930." *The Communist Position on the Negro Question.* New York: Workers Library Publishers, c. 1935. 41–55.

Connor, Walker. *The National Question in Marxist-Leninist Theory and Strategy.* Princeton, N.J.: Princeton University Press, 1984.

Cooley, John. "The Pursuit of the Primitive: Black Portraits by Eugene O'Neill and Other Village Bohemians." *The Harlem Renaissance Re-examined.* Ed. Victor Kramer. New York: AMS, 1987. 51–64.

Cullen, Countee. "Atlantic City Waiter." *Color.* New York: Harper, 1925. 10.

——. *The Black Christ and Other Poems. My Soul's High Song: The Collected Writings of Countee Cullen, Voice of the Harlem Renaissance.* Ed. Gerald Early. New York: Anchor, 1991. 175–236.

——. "Black Majesty." 1929. *My Soul's High Song: The Collected Writings of*

Countee Cullen, Voice of the Harlem Renaissance. Ed. Gerald Early. New York: Anchor, 1991. 200–201.

————. *Copper Sun.* New York: Harper, 1927.

————. "Foreword." *Caroling Dusk: An Anthology of Verse by Negro Poets.* Ed. Countee Cullen. New York: Harper, 1927. ix–xiv.

————. "Fruit of the Flower." *Color.* New York: Harper, 1925. 24–25.

————. "Heritage." *The New Negro.* 1925. Ed. Alain Locke. Introd. Arnold Rampersad. New York: Atheneum, 1992. 250.

————. "Pagan Prayer." *Color.* New York: Harper, 1925. 20–21.

————. "Poet on Poet." *Opportunity* 4 (Feb. 1926): 73–74.

————. "The Shroud of Color." *Color.* New York: Harper, 1925. 26–35.

————. "Yet Do I Marvel." *Color.* New York: Harper, 1925. 3.

Davis, Thadious M. Foreword. *There Is Confusion.* Boston: Northeastern University Press, 1989. v–xxvi.

Dell, Floyd. *Intellectual Vagabondage: An Apology for the Intelligentsia.* New York: Doran, 1926.

Denning, Michael. *The Cultural Front: The Laboring of American Culture in the Twentieth Century.* London: Verso, 1996.

Domingo, W. A. "A New Negro and a New Day." *Messenger* 2.10 (Nov. 1920): 144–45.

Du Bois, W. E. B. "Africa, Colonialism, Zionism." *The Oxford W. E. B. Du Bois Reader.* Ed Eric J. Sundquist. Oxford: Oxford University Press, 1996. 637–40.

————. "The American Scene." *Crisis* 28.1 (May 1924): 7–8.

————. "Awake America." *The Oxford W. E. B. Du Bois Reader.* Ed Eric J. Sundquist. Oxford: Oxford University Press, 1996. 379.

————. "Awake, Put on Thy Strength, O Zion." *Crisis* 16.3 (July 1918): 114.

————. "Class Struggle." *Crisis* 22.4 (Aug. 1921): 151–52.

————. "The Conservation of Races." *The Souls of Black Folk.* Ed. David W. Blight and Robert Gooding-Williams. New York: Bedford, 1997. 228–38.

————. "Forward." *Crisis* 18.5 (Sept. 1919): 234–35.

————. "Judging Russia." *Crisis* 33.4 (Feb. 1927): 189–90.

————. "Little Portraits." *The Oxford W. E. B. Du Bois Reader.* Ed. Eric J. Sundquist. Oxford: Oxford University Press, 1996. 645–47.

———. "Manifesto of the Second Pan-African Congress." Crisis 23.1 (Nov. 1921): 5–10.

———. "The Negro and Radical Thought." Crisis 22.3 (July 1921): 102–4.

———. "The Negro Mind Reaches Out." The New Negro. 1925. Ed. Alain Locke. Introd. Arnold Rampersad. New York: Atheneum, 1992. 385–414.

———. "The Realities in Africa." The Oxford W. E. B. Du Bois Reader. Ed Eric J. Sundquist. Oxford: Oxford University Press, 1996. 653–63.

———. "Socialism and the Negro." Crisis 22.6 (Oct. 1921): 245–47.

———. The Souls of Black Folk. Ed. David W. Blight and Robert Gooding-Williams. New York: Bedford, 1997.

———. "What is Civilization? Africa's Answer." A W. E. B. Du Bois Reader. Ed. Andrew G. Paschal. New York: Macmillan, 1971. 202–10.

Dunjee, Roscoe. "The New Negro." Voices of a Black Nation: Political Journalism in the Harlem Renaissance. Ed. Theodore G. Vincent. Trenton, N.J.: Africa World Press, 1973. 65–66.

Dunne, William F. "Our Party and the Negro Masses." American Communism and Black Americans: A Documentary History. Ed. Philip S. Foner and James S. Allen. Philadelphia: Temple University Press, 1987. 103–5.

Dutt, R. Palme. Fascism and Social Revolution. New York: International Publishers, 1935.

———. The Internationale. London: Lawrence and Wishart, 1964.

Eagleton, Terry. The Ideology of the Aesthetic. Oxford: Basil Blackwell, 1990.

Early, Gerald. Introduction. My Soul's High Song: The Collected Writings of Countee Cullen, Voice of the Harlem Renaissance. Ed. Gerald Early. New York: Anchor, 1991. 3–73.

Eliot, T. S. "Tradition and the Individual Talent." The Critical Tradition: Classic Texts and Contemporary Trends. Ed. David Richter. Boston: Bedford Books, 1998. 498–503.

———. The Waste Land and Other Poems. 1922. New York: Harcourt, 1962.

Elistratova, A. "New Masses." International Literature 1 (1932): 107–14.

Fanon, Frantz. Black Skin, White Masks. Trans. Charles Lam Markmann. New York: Grove, 1967.

———. The Wretched of the Earth. Preface by J. P. Sartre. Trans. Constance Farrington. New York: Grove, 1968.

Fauset, Jesse. "Impressions of the Second Pan-African Congress." *Crisis* 23.1 (Nov. 1921): 12–18.

———. "Nationalism and Egypt." *Crisis* 19.6 (Apr. 1920): 310–16.

———. *Plum Bun.* 1928. Boston: Beacon, 1990.

———. *There Is Confusion.* 1924. Boston: Northeastern University Press, 1989.

Filatova, Lydia. "Langston Hughes: American Writer." *International Literature* 1 (1933): 99–107.

Foley, Barbara. *Radical Representations: Politics and Form in U.S. Proletarian Fiction, 1929–1941.* Durham: Duke University Press, 1993.

Foner, Philip S. *American Socialism and Black Americans: From the Age of Jackson to World War II.* Westport, Conn.: Greenwood, 1977.

Foner, Philip S., and James S. Allen, eds. Introduction. *American Communism and Black Americans: A Documentary History.* Philadelphia: Temple University Press, 1987. vii-xvi.

Ford, James. *The Communists and the Struggle for Negro Liberation: Their Positions on the Problems of Africa, of the West Indies, of War, of Ethiopian Independence, of the Struggle for Peace.* New York: Harlem Division of the Communist Party, c. 1936.

———. "For the Emancipation of Negroes from Imperialism." 1929. *The Communists and the Struggle for Negro Liberation: Their Positions on the Problems of Africa, of the West Indies, of War, of Ethiopian Independence, of the Struggle for Peace.* New York: Harlem Division of the Communist Party, c. 1936. 9–20.

Ford, James W., and James S. Allen. *The Negroes in a Soviet America.* New York: Workers Library Publishers, 1935.

Foster, William Z. *History of the Communist Party of the United States.* New York: International Publishers, 1952.

Flynn, Elizabeth Gurley. "Speech by Elizabeth Gurley Flynn." *Political Affairs* 24.7 (July 1945): 612–18.

Freud, Sigmund. *Beyond the Pleasure Principle.* 1922. New York: W. W. Norton, 1961.

———. *The Ego and the Id.* London: Hogarth, 1962.

———. "Leonardo da Vinci and a Memory of His Childhood." 1910. *The Freud Reader.* Ed. Peter Gay. New York: Norton, 1989. 444–81.

Garvey, Marcus. "Africa for the Africans." *Philosophy and Opinions of Marcus Garvey or Africa for the Africans.* 2 vols. Ed. Amy Jacques Garvey. London: Frank Cass and Co. Ltd., 1967. 50–53.

————. "Capitalism and the State." *Philosophy and Opinions of Marcus Garvey or Africa for the Africans.* 2 vols. Ed. Amy Jacques Garvey. London: Frank Cass and Co. Ltd., 1967. 72–73.

————. "Developing Africa." *The Marcus Garvey and Universal Negro Improvement Association Papers.* Vol. 2. Ed. Robert A. Hill. Berkeley: University of California Press, 1983. 559–60.

————. "History of the Negro." *Philosophy and Opinions of Marcus Garvey or Africa for the Africans.* 2 vols. Ed. Amy Jacques Garvey. London: Frank Cass and Co. Ltd., 1967. 82–83.

————. "The Negro, Communism, Trade Unionism and His (?) Friend." *Philosophy and Opinions of Marcus Garvey or Africa for the Africans.* 2 vols. Ed. Amy Jacques Garvey. London: Frank Cass and Co. Ltd., 1967. 69–73.

————. "Negroes Dig Graves for Each Other Under the Guise of Race Leadership." *Negro World* 28 July 1923: 1.

————. "The Principles of the Universal Negro Improvement Association." *Philosophy and Opinions of Marcus Garvey or Africa for the Africans.* 2 vols. Ed. Amy Jacques Garvey. London: Frank Cass and Co. Ltd., 1967. 93–100.

————. "A Solution for World Peace—1922." *Philosophy and Opinions of Marcus Garvey or Africa for the Africans.* 2 vols. Ed. Amy Jacques Garvey. London: Frank Cass and Co. Ltd., 1967. 31–32.

————. "Speech Delivered at Madison Square Garden, New York City, N.Y., U.S.A., Sunday, March 16, 1924." *Philosophy and Opinions of Marcus Garvey or Africa for the Africans.* 2 vols. Ed. Amy Jacques Garvey. London: Frank Cass and Co. Ltd., 1967. 118–23.

————. "What We Believe." *Philosophy and Opinions of Marcus Garvey or Africa for the Africans.* 2 vols. Ed. Amy Jacques Garvey. London: Frank Cass and Co. Ltd., 1967. 81.

Gates Jr., Henry Luis. *Figures in Black: Words, Signs, and the "Racial" Self.* New York: Oxford University Press, 1987.

————. "Writing, 'Race,' and the Difference It Makes." *The Critical Tradition: Classic Texts and Contemporary Trends.* Ed. David Richter. Boston: Bedford Books, 1998. 1576–88.

Gates Jr., Henry Luis, and Nellie Y. McKay, eds. *The Norton Anthology of African American Literature.* New York: Norton, 1997.

Gellner, Ernest. *Nationalism.* New York: New York University Press, 1997.

Gilroy, Paul. *Against Race: Imagining Political Culture beyond the Color Line.* Cambridge, Mass.: Harvard University Press, 2000.

Gordon, Eugene. "Social and Political Problems of the Negro Writer." *American Writers' Conference.* Ed. Henry Hart. New York: International Publishers, 1935. 141–45.

Gregory, Montgomery. "The Drama of Negro Life." *The New Negro.* 1925. Ed. Alain Locke. Introd. Arnold Rampersad. New York: Atheneum, 1992. 153–60.

Habermas, Jurgen. "The European Nation-state—Its Achievements and Its Limits. On the Past and Future of Sovereignty and Citizenship." *Mapping the Nation.* Ed. Gopal Balakrishnan. London: Verso, 1996. 281–94.

Harding, Warren G. *Messenger* 3.6 (Nov. 1921): 275.

Hart, James D. *The Popular Book: A History of America's Literary Life.* New York: Oxford University Press, 1950.

Haywood, Harry. *Black Bolshevik: Autobiography of an Afro-American Communist.* Chicago: Liberator Press, 1978.

———. "The Crisis of the Jim-Crow Nationalism of the Negro Bourgeoisie." 1931. *American Communism and Black Americans: A Documentary History, 1930–1934.* Ed. Philip S. Foner and Herbert Shapiro. Philadelphia: Temple University Press, 1991. 70–78.

———. "The Theoretical Defenders of White Chauvinism in the Labor Movement." *The Communist Position on the Negro Question.* n.p. c. 1933. 29–40.

Henig, Ruth. *Versailles and After, 1919–1933.* London: Routledge, 1995.

Herskovits, Melville J. "The Negro's Americanism." *The New Negro.* 1925. Ed. Alain Locke. Introd. Arnold Rampersad. New York: Atheneum, 1992. 353–60.

Hill, Patricia Liggins, ed. *Call and Response: The Riverside Anthology of the African American Literary Tradition.* New York: Houghton Mifflin, 1998.

Hobsbawm, E. J. *The Age of Extremes: A History of the World, 1914–1991.* New York: Vintage, 1996.

———. *Nations and Nationalism Since 1780: Programme, Myth, Reality.* Cambridge: Cambridge University Press, 1993.

Hroch, Miroslav. "From National Movement to the Fully-formed Nation: The Nation-building Process in Europe." *Mapping the Nation.* Ed. Gopal Balakrishnan. London: Verso, 1996. 78–97.

Huggins, Nathan Irvin. Introduction. *Voices From the Harlem Renaissance.* Ed.

Nathan Irvin Huggins. New York: Oxford University Press, 1976. 3–11.

———. *Harlem Renaissance*. London: Oxford University Press, 1971.

Hughes, Langston. "Advertisement for the Waldorf-Astoria." *The Collected Poems of Langston Hughes*. Ed. Arnold Rampersad. New York: Vintage, 1995. 143–46.

———. "Air Raid over Harlem." *The Collected Poems of Langston Hughes*. Ed. Arnold Rampersad. New York: Random, 1994. 185–88.

———. "Always the Same." *The Collected Poems of Langston Hughes*. Ed. Arnold Rampersad. New York: Random, 1994. 165–66.

———. *The Big Sea*. New York: Knopf, 1940.

———. "Chant for May Day." *A New Song*. *The Collected Poems of Langston Hughes*. Ed. Arnold Rampersad. New York: Random, 1994. 209–10.

———. "Concerning Red Baiting." *Good Morning Revolution: Uncollected Writings of Langston Hughes*. Ed. Faith Berry. New York: Carol Publishing Group, 1992. 159–61.

———. "Danse Africaine." *The Weary Blues*. New York: Knopf, 1926. 105.

———. "Death in Harlem." *The Collected Poems of Langston Hughes*. Ed. Arnold Rampersad. New York: Random, 1994. 179–83.

———. "Dream Variation." *The Weary Blues*. New York: Knopf, 1926. 43.

———. "Epilogue." *The Weary Blues*. New York: Knopf, 1926. 109.

———. *Fine Clothes to the Jew*. New York: Knopf, 1927.

———. "Good Morning, Revolution." *The Collected Poems of Langston Hughes*. Ed. Arnold Rampersad. New York: Random, 1994. 162–63.

———. "I Too." *The New Negro*. 1925. Ed. Alain Locke. Introd. Arnold Rampersad. New York: Atheneum, 1992. 145.

———. "Johannesburg Mines." *The Collected Poems of Langston Hughes*. Ed. Arnold Rampersad. New York: Vintage, 1995. 43.

———. "Lament for Dark Peoples." *The Weary Blues*. New York: Knopf, 1926. 100.

———. "Langston Hughes Speaks." *Good Morning Revolution: Uncollected Writings of Langston Hughes*. Ed. Faith Berry. New York: Carol Publishing Group, 1992. 157–59.

———. "Let America Be America Again." *The Collected Poems of Langston Hughes*. Ed. Arnold Rampersad. New York: Random, 1994. 189–91.

———. "Letter from Spain." *The Collected Poems of Langston Hughes*. Ed. Arnold Rampersad. New York: Random, 1994. 201–2.

———. "Merry Christmas." *The Collected Poems of Langston Hughes*. Ed. Arnold Rampersad. New York: Random, 1994. 132.

———. "My Adventures as a Social Poet." *Good Morning Revolution: Uncollected Writings of Langston Hughes*. Ed. Faith Berry. New York: Carol Publishing Group, 1992. 150–57.

———. "The Negro Artist and the Racial Mountain." *Voices From the Harlem Renaissance*. Ed. Nathan Irvin Huggins. New York: Oxford University Press, 1976. 305–9.

———. "The Negro Speaks of Rivers." *The New Negro*. 1925. Ed. Alain Locke. Introd. Arnold Rampersad. New York: Atheneum, 1992. 141.

———. "The Negro Troops." *Fighting Words*. Ed. Donald Ogden Stewart. New York: Harcourt, 1940. 58–63.

———. "One More 'S' in the U.S.A." *The Collected Poems of Langston Hughes*. Ed. Arnold Rampersad. New York: Random, 1994. 176–77.

———. "Open Letter to the South." *The Collected Poems of Langston Hughes*. Ed. Arnold Rampersad. New York: Random, 1994. 160–61.

———. "Our Land." *The Weary Blues*. New York: Knopf, 1926. 99.

———. "Poem." *The Weary Blues*. New York: Knopf, 1926. 58.

———. "Proem." *The Weary Blues*. New York: Knopf, 1926. 19.

———. *Scottsboro Limited: Four Poems and a Play in Verse*. New York: Golden Stair Press, 1932.

———. "Sister Johnson Marches." *The Collected Poems of Langston Hughes*. Ed. Arnold Rampersad. New York: Random, 1994. 197.

———. "Song for a Banjo Dance." *The Weary Blues*. New York: Knopf, 1926. 36.

———. "Song for Ourselves." *The Collected Poems of Langston Hughes*. Ed. Arnold Rampersad. New York: Random, 1994. 207.

———. "Steel Mills." *The Collected Poems of Langston Hughes*. Ed. Arnold Rampersad. New York: Vintage, 1995. 43.

———. "To Midnight Nan at Leroy's." *The Weary Blues*. New York: Knopf, 1926. 30.

———. "To Negro Writers." *American Writers' Conference*. Ed. Henry Hart. New York: International Publishers, 1935. 139–41.

———. "Too Much of Race." *Good Morning Revolution: Uncollected Writings of Langston Hughes*. Ed. Faith Berry. New York: Carol Publishing Group, 1992. 101–4.

————. "White Man." *The Collected Poems of Langston Hughes.* Ed. Arnold Rampersad. New York: Random, 1994. 194–95.

Hutchinson, Earl Ofari. *Blacks and Reds: Race and Class in Conflict, 1919–1990.* East Lansing: Michigan State University Press, 1995.

JanMohamed, Abdul. "Negating the Negation as a Form of Affirmation in Minority Discourse: The Construction of Richard Wright as Subject." *Richard Wright: A Collection of Critical Essays.* Ed. Arnold Rampersad. Englewood Cliffs, N.J.: Prentice Hall, 1995. 107–23.

Johnson, James Weldon. *The Book of American Negro Poetry.* 1922. New York: Harcourt, Brace & World, 1958.

————. "Harlem: The Culture Capital." *The New Negro.* 1925. Ed. Alain Locke. Introd. Arnold Rampersad. New York: Atheneum, 1992. 301–11.

Kelley, Robin D. G. *Hammer and Hoe: Alabama Communists During the Great Depression.* Chapel Hill: University of North Carolina Press, 1990.

————. *Race Rebels: Culture, Politics and the Black Working Class.* New York: Macmillan, 1994.

Kellogg, Paul U. "The Negro Pioneers." *The New Negro.* 1925. Ed. Alain Locke. Introd. Arnold Rampersad. New York: Atheneum, 1992. 271–77.

Klein, Melanie. "Love, Guilt and Reparation." 1937. *Love, Hate and Reparation.* New York: W. W. Norton, 1964. 57–119.

Kornweibel, Theodore. *Seeing Red: Federal Campaigns Against Black Militancy, 1919–1925.* Bloomington: Indiana University Press, 1998.

Lawson, Elizabeth. Introduction. *The Communist Position on the Negro Question.* n.p. c. 1933. 1–2.

Lenin, V. I. "Preliminary Draft of Theses on the National and Colonial Questions." *Lenin on the National and Colonial Questions: Three Articles.* Peking: Foreign Languages Press, 1970. 20–29.

————. "The Socialist Revolution and the Right of Nations to Self-Determination." *Lenin on the National and Colonial Questions: Three Articles.* Peking: Foreign Languages Press, 1970. 1–19.

Lewis, David Levering. *When Harlem Was in Vogue.* 1979. New York: Oxford University Press, 1989.

Locke, Alain. "Art or Propaganda." 1928. *The Critical Temper of Alain Locke: A Selection of His Essays on Art and Culture.* Ed. Jeffrey C. Stewart. New York: Garland, 1983. 27–28.

———. "The Concept of Race as Applied to Social Culture." 1924. *The Philosophy of Alain Locke: Harlem Renaissance and Beyond*. Ed. Leonard Harris. Philadelphia: Temple University Press, 1989. 187–99.

———. "The Negro Spirituals." *The New Negro*. 1925. Ed. Alain Locke. Introd. Arnold Rampersad. New York: Atheneum, 1992. 199–213.

———. "Negro Youth Speaks." *The New Negro*. 1925. Ed. Alain Locke. Introd. Arnold Rampersad. New York: Atheneum, 1992. 47–53.

———. "The New Negro." *The New Negro*. 1925. Ed. Alain Locke. Introd. Arnold Rampersad. New York: Atheneum, 1992. 3–16.

———. *The New Negro: An Interpretation*. New York: Boni, 1925.

———. "Our Little Renaissance." 1927. *The Critical Temper of Alain Locke: A Selection of His Essays on Art and Culture*. Ed. Jeffrey C. Stewart. New York: Garland, 1983. 21–22.

———. "Racial Progress and Race Adjustment." 1915. *Race Contact and Interracial Relations: Lectures on the Theory and Practice of Race*. Ed. Jeffrey C. Stewart. Washington, D.C.: Howard University Press, 1992. 84–104.

Lukács, Georg. "'Tendency' or Partisanship?" 1932. *Essays on Realism*. Cambridge, Mass.: MIT, 1980. 33–44.

Martin, Tony. *Literary Garveyism: Garvey, Black Arts, and the Harlem Renaissance*. Dover, Mass: Majority Press, 1983.

Marx, Karl. *The Communist Manifesto*. *Ten Classics of Marxism*. New York: International Publishers, 1940.

Maxwell, William J. *New Negro, Old Left: African-American Writing and Communism Between the Wars*. New York: Columbia University Press, 1999.

McKay, Claude. "Adolescence." 1922. *The Passion of Claude McKay: Selected Poetry and Prose, 1912–1948*. Ed. Wayne F. Cooper. New York: Schocken, 1973. 120.

———. "Birds of Prey." *Messenger* 2.2 (Dec. 1919): 23.

———. *Constab Ballads*. London: Watts, 1912.

———. "Enslaved." 1921. *The Passion of Claude McKay: Selected Poetry and Prose, 1912–1948*. Ed. Wayne F. Cooper. New York: Schocken, 1973. 121.

———. "Flame-Heart." *The Passion of Claude McKay: Selected Poetry and Prose, 1912–1948*. Ed. Wayne F. Cooper. New York: Schocken, 1973. 118.

———. "Garvey as a Negro Moses." 1922. *The Passion of Claude McKay: Selected Poetry and Prose, 1912–1948*. Ed. Wayne F. Cooper. New York: Schocken, 1973. 65–69.

———. *Home to Harlem*. New York: Harper and Bros., 1928.

————. "How Black Sees Green and Red." 1921. *The Passion of Claude McKay: Selected Poetry and Prose, 1912–1948.* Ed. Wayne F. Cooper. New York: Schocken, 1973. 57–62.

————. "In Bondage." 1920. *The Passion of Claude McKay: Selected Poetry and Prose, 1912–1948.* Ed. Wayne F. Cooper. New York: Schocken, 1973. 122.

————. *Negroes in America.* 1922. Trans. Robert J. Winter. Ed. Alan L. McLeod. Port Washington, N.Y.: Kennikat, 1979.

————. "Outcast." 1922. *The Passion of Claude McKay: Selected Poetry and Prose, 1912–1948.* Ed. Wayne F. Cooper. New York: Schocken, 1973. 121.

————. "Socialism and the Negro." 1920. *The Passion of Claude McKay: Selected Poetry and Prose, 1912–1948.* Ed. Wayne F. Cooper. New York: Schocken, 1973. 50–54.

————. *Songs of Jamaica.* Kingston, Jamaica: Aston W. Gardner, 1912.

————. "The Tropics of New York." 1920. *The Passion of Claude McKay: Selected Poetry and Prose, 1912–1948.* Ed. Wayne F. Cooper. New York: Schocken, 1973. 117.

————. "White Houses." *The New Negro.* 1925. Ed. Alain Locke. Introd. Arnold Rampersad. New York: Atheneum, 1992. 134.

Miller, Kelly. "The Harvest of Race Prejudice." 1925. *Survey Graphic: Harlem, Mecca of the New Negro.* Baltimore: Black Classic Press, 1980. 682–83, 711–12. Rpt. of *Survey Graphic: Harlem, Mecca of the New Negro* 6.6 (Mar. 1925).

————. "Howard: The National Negro University." *The New Negro.* 1925. Ed. Alain Locke. Introd. Arnold Rampersad. New York: Atheneum, 1992. 312–22.

Miller, Lelia V. "Wake Up, Sleeping Africa!" *Negro World* 29 Dec. 1923: 6.

Minor, Robert. "Death of a Program!" 1926. *American Communism and Black Americans: A Documentary History, 1919–1929.* Philadelphia: Temple University Press, 1987. 136–41.

Mokhtar, G. Introduction. *UNESCO General History of Africa Vol. II: AncientCivilizations of Africa.* Ed. G. Mokhtar. London: Heinemann, 1981. 1–23.

Moses, Wilson Jeremiah. "More Stately Mansions: New Negro Movements and Langston Hughes' Literary Theory." *Langston Hughes Review* 4.1 (Spring 1985): 40–46.

Moton, Robert R. "Hampton-Tuskegee: Missioners of the Masses." *The*

New Negro. 1925. Ed. Alain Locke. Introd. Arnold Rampersad. New York: Atheneum, 1992. 323–32.

Mullen, Bill V. "Breaking the Signifying Chain: A New Blueprint for African-American Literary Studies." *Modern Fiction Studies* 47.1 (Spring 2001): 145–63.

———. *Popular Fronts: Chicago and African-American Cultural Politics, 1935–1946.* Urbana: University of Illinois Press, 1999.

Murphy, James A. *The Proletarian Moment: The Controversy Over Leftism in Literature.* Urbana: University of Illinois Press, 1991.

Olgin. M. J. *Why Communism? Plain Talks on Vital Problems.* San Francisco: Western Worker Publishers, 1934.

Oneal, James. "The Next Emancipation." *Messenger* 4.6 (June 1922): 420–21.

Owen, Chandler, and A. Philip Randolph. "The Menace of Negro Communists." *Messenger* 5.8 (Aug. 1923): 784.

———. "The New Negro—What Is He?" *Messenger* 2.7 (Aug. 1920): 73–74.

———. "The New Patriotism." *Messenger* 1.3 (Mar. 1919): 26.

———. "The Peace Treaty." *Messenger* 1.8 (Aug. 1919): 5.

Painter, Nell. *The Narrative of Hosea Hudson, His Life as a Negro Communist in the South.* Cambridge: Harvard University Press, 1979.

Parham, E. Saydee. "Woman's Part in Building Nationhood." *The Negro World* Nov. 1924: 8.

Patterson, William. "Awake Negro Poets!" *New Masses* 4 (Oct. 1928): 10.

Peters, Paul, and George Sklar. *Stevedore: A Play in Three Acts.* New York: Covici-Friede, 1934.

Rampersad, Arnold. *The Art and Imagination of W. E. B. Du Bois.* Cambridge, Mass.: Harvard University Press, 1976.

———. "Introduction." *The New Negro.* 1925. Ed. Alain Locke. New York: Atheneum, 1992. ix-xxiii.

———. "Langston Hughes and His Critics on the Left." *Langston Hughes Review* 5.2 (1986): 34–40.

Randolph, A. Philip. "Black Zionism." *Messenger* 4.1 (Jan. 1922): 330–35.

———. "Garveyism." *Messenger* 3.4 (Sept. 1921): 248–52.

———. "The Only Way to Redeem Africa." *Messenger* 4.11 (Nov. 1922): 522–24.

————. "The Only Way to Redeem Africa." *Messenger* 4.12 (Dec. 1922): 540–42.

————. "The Only Way to Redeem Africa." *Messenger* 5.1 (Jan. 1923): 568–70.

————. "The Only Way to Redeem Africa." *Messenger* 5.2 (Feb. 1923): 612–14.

Rogers, J. A. "Jazz at Home." *The New Negro*. 1925. Ed. Alain Locke. Introd. Arnold Rampersad. New York: Atheneum, 1992. 216–24.

Schatz, Philip. "Songs of the Negro Worker." *New Masses* May 1930: 6.

Schomberg, Arthur. "The Negro Digs Up His Past." *The New Negro*. 1925. Ed. Alain Locke. Introd. Arnold Rampersad. New York: Atheneum, 1992. 231–37.

Scruggs, Charles W. "Alain Locke and Walter White: Their Struggle for Control of the Harlem Renaissance." *Black American Literature Forum* 14.3 (Fall 1980): 91–99.

Skerrett, Joseph T. "Composing Bigger: Wright and the Making of *Native Son*." *Critical Essays on Richard Wright's* Native Son. Ed. Keneth Kinnamon. New York: G. K. Hall, 1997. 104–18.

Simons, William. *Hands Off Cuba*. New York: Workers Library Publishers, 1933.

Smethurst, James Edward. *The New Red Negro: The Literary Left and African American Poetry, 1930–1946*. New York: Oxford University Press, 1999.

Smith, Rochelle, and Sharon L. Jones, eds. *The Prentice Hall Anthology of African American Literature*. Upper Saddle River, N.J.: Prentice Hall, 2000.

Stalin, Joseph. *Marxism and the National and Colonial Question: Selected Writings and Speeches*. New York: International Publishers, 1942.

Stewart, Jeffrey Conrad. Introduction. *Race Contacts and Interracial Relations: Lectures on the Theory and Practice of Race*. By Alain LeRoy Locke. Washington, D.C.: Howard University Press, 1992. xix-lix.

Stokes, Rose Pastor. "The Cause of Freedom: Blacks and Communists." *Voices of a Black Nation: Political Journalism in the Harlem Renaissance*. Ed. Theodore G. Vincent. Trenton, N.J.: Africa World Press, 1973. 130–36.

————. "The Communist International and the Negro." 1923. *American Communism and Black Americans: A Documentary History, 1919–1929*. Philadelphia: Temple University Press, 1987. 30–32.

Sundquist, Eric J. "The Concept of Race." *The Oxford W. E. B. Du Bois Reader*. Ed. Eric J. Sundquist. Oxford: Oxford University Press, 1996. 37–38.

Taylor, Harry. "Of Africa." *Negro World* 19 May 1923: 6.

Taylor, Theman Ray. "Cyril Briggs and the African Blood Brotherhood: Another Radical View of Race and Class During the 1920s." Diss., University of California, Santa Barbara, 1981.

Tillery, Tyrone. *Claude McKay: A Poet's Struggle for Identity*. Amherst: University of Massachusetts Press, 1992.

Toomer, Jean. "Georgia Dusk." *The New Negro*. 1925. Ed. Alain Locke. Introd. Arnold Rampersad. New York: Atheneum, 1992. 136.

Tracy, Steven C. *Langston Hughes and the Blues*. Urbana: University of Illinois Press, 1988.

Trani, Eugene P., and David L. Wilson. *The Presidency of Warren G. Harding*. Lawrence: Regents Press of Kansas, 1977.

U.N.I.A. "Report of UNIA Parade." *The Marcus Garvey and Universal Negro Improvement Association Papers*. Vol. 2. Ed. Robert A. Hill. Berkeley: University of California Press, 1983. 490–94.

———. "The Universal Ethiopian Anthem." *The Marcus Garvey and Universal Negro Improvement Association Papers*. Vol. 2. Ed. Robert A. Hill. Berkeley: University of California Press, 1983. 575–76.

Weiss, Henry George. "Americanism." *New Masses* 1 Jan. 1935: 6.

Williams, Raymond. *The Country and the City*. New York: Oxford University Press, 1973.

———. *Marxism and Literature*. New York: Oxford University Press, 1985.

Wright, Richard. "American Negroes in Key Posts of Spain's Loyalist Forces." *Daily Worker* 29 Sept. 1937: 2.

———. *Black Boy*. New York: HarperPerennial, 1993.

———. "Blueprint for Negro Writing." *Within the Circle: An Anthology of African American Literary Criticism from the Harlem Renaissance to the Present*. Ed. Angelyn Mitchell. Durham: Duke University Press, 1994. 97–106.

———. "Born A Slave, She Recruits 5 Members For Communist Party." *Daily Worker* 30 Aug. 1937: 3.

———. "Harlem Spanish Women Come Out of the Kitchen." *Daily Worker* 20 Sept. 1937: 5.

———. "How Bigger Was Born." *Native Son*. 1940. New York: HarperPerennial, 1993. 505–40.

———. "James W. Ford Celebrates 44th Birthday—Leads Progressives in Harlem Community." *Daily Worker* 23 Dec. 1937: 4.

———. *Lawd Today!* 1963. Boston: Northeastern University Press, 1993.

————. "Mrs. Holmes and Daughters Drink From the Fountain of Communism." *Daily Worker* 7 Sept. 1937: 5.

————. *Native Son.* 1940. New York: HarperPerennial, 1993.

————. "Negro Social Worker Hails Housing, Education in Spain." *Daily Worker* 12 Nov. 1937: 2.

————. "Negro Writers Launch Literary Quarterly." *Daily Worker* 8 June 1937: 7.

————. "Negro Youth On March, Says Leader." *Daily Worker* 7 Oct. 1937: 3.

————. "Pullman Porters to Celebrate 12th Year of Their Union." *Daily Worker* 19 Aug. 1937: 3.

————. *12 Million Black Voices.* 1941. New York: Thunder's Mouth Press, 1988.

————. *Uncle Tom's Children.* 1940. New York: HarperPerennial, 1993.

————. "Walter Garland Tells What Spain's Fight Against Fascism Means to the Negro People." *Daily Worker* 29 Nov. 1937: 2.